Karolinum Press

Bohuslav Reynek
The Well at Morning

MODERN
CZECH
CLASSICS

Bohuslav Reynek

THE WELL AT MORNING

*Selected Poems
and Graphic Artworks,
1925–1971*

Translated from the Czech by Justin Quinn

With essays by Martin C. Putna,
Justin Quinn, and Jiří Šerých

Karolinum Press

This book was kindly supported by the Ministry of Culture
of the Czech Republic.

ISBN 978-80-246-3425-8 (pb)
ISBN 978-80-246-3426-5 (ebk)

ABOUT THE AUTHOR

Bohuslav Reynek (1892–1971) was born in the village of Petrkov, in the Czech-Moravian Highlands. He translated widely from French and German literature and began writing poetry in the 1910s, publishing his first book in 1921. During this period he was part of the Roman Catholic apocalyptic sect run by Josef Florian, and while the fervor of these early years would wane, Reynek would remain a Christian to his death. He was also an artist, and his etchings and engravings are remarkable for the manner in which they combine religious themes with detailed observation of his immediate rural surroundings. In 1926 he married the French poet Suzanne Renaud, with whom he had two sons. From the late 1920s to the beginning of World War II, they divided the year between Czechoslovakia and her home town of Grenoble. After the Communist putsch of 1948, Reynek's farmstead was taken from him, and he and his sons were reassigned to it as day laborers by the authorities. While always well-known as a translator, it was not until the 1960s that his importance as both a poet and artist become more widely recognized. This is the first appearance of Reynek's work in English in book form.

CONTENTS

SELECTED POEMS

SELECTED POEMS

A FOOL

In my village, I'm the fool.
Sad dogs know me – sad white school
of sleepy dogs that drift away
into the distance. They don't bay.
They keep me happy from afar –
cloudish dogs is what they are
that run about the sky's massif.
And we're all drunk on grief.
Where we wander we don't know.
Ancient shepherd, as I go,
bless my soul with your great gifts
of moon and these long wakeful shifts,
heavy, gashed time and again
like a bleeding heart. Amen.

SIGNS OF AUTUMN

September's here again, sweetening my blood
again like wine. Lament, a quiet flood,
grows in my heart: rosehips grow ever redder,
hundreds of hearts. And so my soul can better
rest when the labour of the harvest's quit,
a hazy veil of fire comes down on it
like a sudarium of spider webs.
Dawn flames my face in silence, and night ebbs.
My mouth is parched for it – the wounds deep –
and begs: O Lord, this late summer will
my soul, a swallow blue, rise steep
in air and fly to new lands, dipping its bill
along the way to sip from seas of peace?
And with each word my blood is sweetened further.

HOAR-FROST

Weary autumn pastures. Down they sink,
and butterflies stiff with cold now drink
dawn's dew.

Lifting their wings. They can no longer fly –
a nacreous green on flowers sealed-up and dry,
they flame.

I, too, am tired. A mushroom on the wayside
crimped white like folds of fabric on a bride –
I pick

and peel it. Hand is scented rich and sere.
My heart is heavier than it was last year,
with love.

I peel it. Scent. And then I see white flocks
in my soul's eye, and tending this livestock
is autumn.

So clean and good and early, autumn stands,
fixing on its head with icy strands
a veil.

SPRINGTIDE

A chaffinch in a tree
of cherry sings merrily
spring's *introit*.

Its blazing bobble dwells
in leaves, alive, and swells
in scarlet.

The flowers are flares of white.
The chaffinch has gone quiet
and turned sky-gazer.

My eyes close on the day:
an orb revolves in grey
and red and azure.

Russet, it radiates,
emerging from the straits
of pain's blood-tide.

I want it, here amidst
these canopies of bliss,
ungratified.

BALLAD

On my outstretched palm a strange guest has landed.
A kind of dove? A crystal smoothly sanded?

Is it some milky quartz? Perhaps a lark
that has alighted, radiance in this dark?

An owl that gazes burns, soft plume on plume?
Bewilderment that streams from poppy bloom?

No. It is the fruit of the serpent's tree.
Eve placed it on the palm, unhappily.

Fruit of my death, blessed by a cross, this host
is very hard and Satan fears it most.

THE MORNING...

The morning shows a dove in shade,
white as a new egg, passing fairness.
And then amidst the lengths of hair-grass
a hare that hides in the frosted glade,

master of scent, in misted wold.
These two have set the blood on fire.
The wailing of the blood sings higher,
caught by the heart that ails with cold.

Two consolations thus colliding,
like slender mirrors. Figures traded,
a rose burst from them, and then faded
in rays of light that scorch and frighten;

its sparks that fly, that cobwebs catch,
this rose consumed in air now warm,
now fire that has no face or form –
fire, most merciful Jack Ketch.

PILGRIMAGE TO LA SALETTE

Green freshet, happy boon,
becomes your brother soon;
the wildlife's scent in leas;
haws, black thorns and beech trees;
small flowers, their names unknown,
wedged long ago in stone,
quietly, their flames brightening.
The sky is chaliced lightning,
and autumn earth is gold
and red leaves on the wold.
Steam rises in the blue.
The hills below Obiou,
(now aged and white) are steep.
With us: the cattle, sheep,
a dog, two mules, a maid,
partridges in the glade...
A holy mount for prayer,
the church door open. Go there,
the chilling grief, the ache.
And in Our Lady's wake
(or rather that of light
in whose veils flowering white
a moon in mist's wide lake),
tar reeks and blackly blooms;
clean humble earth resumes
its shape – her prints are gone.
To your woe they lead on.
Eternal, exposed crest,
this Virgin's fort be blessed.

DAWN IN WINTER

The gloom. Small light the lamp releases,
in ash-grey fog, damask and white.
The rhythm of the silence eases
the lamp off like a boat, in light.

My drowsy thought can't tell at all
where it might find and have its fill;
it searches for at least a wall
to steady itself for a while.

Here only is the fruit's light gold,
and here the strong wall is the frost.
Mint scents the bread of hope's each fold –
the motte, the keep that can't be lost.

At this so gently through the glass
dawn comes. A limpid soul it stands.
It puts a rose into my vase
and pours some blood upon my hands.

We laid out food upon our board
in praise of what is wildly chaste;
ironic cloth – its shadow horde
as cold as lips that have death's taste.

IDYLL, MORNING

The white ox in the yard
looks up into the dawn
(the byre remains bestarred),
and sees moist florets drawn,

small dreams, from deepest night,
from hidden paths, the roll
of meadows slack with quiet
that sate and that console,

across the warm, dark span
of autumn-time's oak wolds.
With him a sloven man
lights up the place in gold.

With him a drunk, in age
(perhaps once sad as well,
and now these muses' mage),
strikes gold – a match's spell

of comfort. Cigarette.
Smoke, angels, and lemurs...
– Votive, no sheen of sweat,
the white ox, beaten, stirs.

And stares skywards, his duty
to see the lies there laded.
With him we dream of beauty,
which held us, and then faded.

MID-WINTER LONGING

A gust sends tremors through my dreams,
a butterfly in cobweb beams;

across the waters, longing goes,
across the fish, the shores, the snows,

and spears me at this year's extreme,
a spider and its cobweb beams.

I'm woven in this net so deep.
January gets me drunk with sleep,

and its ice wine of sleep is worst –
the shoulders and the head it hurts,

the heart... No tang of wine to it.
Perhaps it's dust mixed in with spit,

to cleanse the soul in Siloam's dew,
so it can see and in a new

light net end up and newly gaze,
this hard and solitary blaze,

this lamp a sponge, its every bleb
is vinegar – cob into its web.

THREE GOATS

White kids rise from the hay,
like foam upon a play
of waters; they look round sweetly,
a triple moon couched neatly
in heaven green, so bright;
such tiny cloudlets white,
or trusting angels fair
that rise into the air,
good marvels beautiful...
They frisk, they push and pull,
then head to hip they lie.
Tomorrow's *Oculi*.
Their rounds are a retrieval,
their tenderness primeval –
the light of Isaac, blind,
his blessèd seed and kind.
Great flowering mysteries.
The lush glow they release
amidst the gloomy sties
fills my dim, bleary eyes,
and now they usher in
the mundane in a vision.

COCKERELS

Cockerels proudly roam –
the sun for their heads' comb.
They rise from night dew's rinse
in purple, fold on fold,
and strut about the yard –
speckled, ashen, gold,
and black – each one a lord
of daybreak, and with powers
to bless the dawn, panache
of paths and gates and towers.
These wardens – Petrine, brash
and awful – guard the sties.
They taunt grand distant ranks,
cut others down to size –
such fornicating swanks,
such evil gold-eyed gods
on tribunals of trash,
guffawing at all odds,
these wardens – Petrine, brash –
patrons of dawn's despair,
with loud and savage airs,
with bugles and alarums
of sin they hound so well,
echoing Satan's charms
and laughter when they yell
across the plains of hell.

CARPENTERS IN THE WIND

Cold wind rakes me with its excess.
These carpenters with their axes,
darkly working deeper,
close-fisted, slender reapers,
bad jokes and curses even cheaper,
they cut the tree.

They lop the head from off the wind.
It grows once more from its neck;
just blood comes rushing without check
from its mouth. Their carpentry
destroys this beautiful tree,
this fragrant tree all white,
and cold wind howls its blight
in my heart like, again,
these men
with their axes.

I've lost one of my own.
I'm more and more alone.
These men have finished chopping.
My bitter heart so rails,
like a dog that rolls in chippings,
in chippings purple-flecked, it wails.

HAIR

Lush foliage of skulls
sweet flood of blood that spills,
ashen, blonde and jet,
you robe a woman's head,
concealing like conceits
that poets' dreaming breeds.
You primal want in waves
that whips and flaming chafes,
panache of women's bones.
You smoke that swirls and moans.
You wondrous flowers of flesh
whose heavy perfumes thresh
with want through cleft and vise.
You hair, swarm of slight flies.
You writhing worms of sin,
the bonds of will so thin.
You needles poisoned, soft
in gold and silvercraft.
The oils around your reins
lead me down what dark lanes?
Nets spread wide as snares,
so lips catch fire. You flares,
you glints of blue and red
from which such tears have bled,
and carved the face with lines.
You ivy, climbing vine
on Purgatory's wall,
from what depths do you call?

SPIDER

He crawled out of a crack,
this guilt – eight-legged, black,
small star. All abdomen,
above a soft wall, flaxen
clapboard hovel. Round here,
spoilt in this quiet byre,
these are tame. I love them,
dusky thieves, no stem
of neck, outcasts, outlaws,
birds with sly wings (because
you see them sweetly glide
in autumn, side to side).
Of filamented flowers
the author, bright in dark bowers,
white webs from slat to post,
wreathes of a banished ghost;
grey drapes... The silkiest,
soft hammock, it lures the guest
to sleep in creviced stalls
with carpets. It enthralls
its lord who waits in dust,
death's navel, spider, ballast
deft, a black seed pod
sprung from this cursèd clod
of earth. Small toad, so spry
and poison, powder dry.
This guilt – eight-legged, black.
My henbane eyes gaze back.

FLY

On my white clothes it lights,
itself forthwith ignites,
green-gold, in silence – fly
that augurs how all die.
Strange glow in fabric's fold,
flower-jewel and rose of mold.
Legs, head, and wings prepare
like Jack Ketch; then despair
the victims. Night rainbow shines,
no sun, a glass of wine,
green crystal, cruel and hard,
safely keeps it guard.
Loyal follower of feasts,
the kind of unclean beasts,
I nurse it in my bosom.
But eyes feed on this blossom,
the waves in webs that weave,
with interest, gibes, and grief.
I've killers at my behest
(fingers to crush the guest);
but I might stay reflecting
upon the stomach I reckon
heart-like, beautiful, fecund.

GATHERING POTATOES

This crop in clay, so humble, shines.
Out of the ploughed-up earth a breeze:
these give themselves up to the tines,
and from the furrow a fullness breathes.

The farmhands trail behind red cows
and rake through varicolored golds.
White weave of winter around the ploughs
lifts off late-summer haulms in folds.

Goats search for grass and the dog plays
about the field that we put drills in.
Above our heads peace is ablaze.
The father cannot hear his children.

And in the hayrick's shade are stored
two jugs and bread carefully wrapped
in cloth that's blue to please our Lord –
for us the brown, broken, and chapped.

YELLOW BEDSTRAW, A BLESSING

In muddy ditches dried,
gold smoke, the ground ablaze,
the bedstraw is cast wide,
boiled up in these scorched days,

for the solitary dove,
the herds on fallow lands,
from earth's deep trove
the dead reach up their hands.

SNOW ACROSS THE THRESHOLD

What angel at the door
slips in so white a sheet?
I read it, looking for
the pain that it will mete.

I read it. Of stars no hint.
Snow on the village falling.
With Christ-tide its lanes glint,
forgetting then recalling.

Joy fills the doorway now.
Star prints of Paradise –
letters strewn anyhow
a bird leaves as it flies.

THE WELL AT MORNING

The table's touched by dawn,
pierced palm of the just fate,
some light, some joy in-borne.
The well hums near the gate.

A fate at her dark weft
beside the well this morning,
she mercifully tries the heft
of reproach and of warning.

She calls the soul from dreams.
Unasking, she replies.
Above the springs of streams
memory's suffering eyes.

Hunched under the dark's robe
she rises and takes hold.
And for wounds of which Job
does she steep these cloths cold?

HAWKMOTHS AT EVENING

The dust path like a brand.
The dark joins hands. And quick
resplendent hawkmoths land
on windows grey as brick.

A plea sinks on night's sill –
such longing and such hurry.
And peace, a forest well,
speaks out of your long worry.

From bends of clouds are blown
these deathly lilies, blooming.
Cursed gift of gold, just one,
the far moon gives, illuming.

Thus peace at evening time
plights death with these great flocks.
Street windows, graves in line,
this key of fire unlocks.

LIGHT BREEZE

Beneath the trees the foliage mills –
murmuring hordes,
my last and golden flock. Which hills
do you rush towards?

Gold flock and lambs in blood immersed –
whose sacrifice?
On this death-stone who of us first
into mist flies?

What shepherd likes to leave his herd?
What herd his crook?
Who slips away from whom through swards
of mist and smoke?

INITIALS

On sleepless nights, to take the missal
and leaf through it is sweet, to mark
where you have found peace's initial
and stared till it glowed from the dark.

Is this the moon with stars, the 'o'
of Omega, bright edge of haze,
a branch above us lined with snow,
the mist upon the leas

from which paths like an Alpha wake,
the initial spread unhindered
in silence over burn and brake,
a memory of winter?

EVENING

In the farmyard, where we are lost,
so large, dark after dusk,
the children chase with lights that cross
the goats' leaf trash and husks.

The path's from here, though magic hides it.
Perhaps the scent of sprays
that fell in frost will help us find it,
frost that shone in sun-rays.

The children's footfalls scatter sparks
through dried-up leaves. They spread
like words of songs. And from our dark
some words can now be read.

SHADOWS

Cobwebs wound round the empty swallows' nests
(the morning's redness taken by their wings).
The blackened lamp whispers and attests
to darkness falling and to brightenings.

The byre at morning. Darkness rich with gleam.
A glint of head-brass, cribs, some wood beyond.
Shadows and lights cleave to the cattle team.
They are like calves, their bodies dunned and blonde.

Beside black troughs, they lie down in the straw.
They huddle even closer with their mates
to the sound of milk: its froth and bubbles draw
the ginger cat, which licks her fur and waits.

Darkness. A lamp in it. The pillars start
to fade and shadow edges almost glisten.
Mortal eyes can hardly tell apart
what is the earth and what already isn't.

NOVEMBER

Through the land November strays,
a sorrel horse with a white blaze.

He stretches past the wooded hills,
a mane of rushes rustles still.

He rears up high above the trees,
his blaze of snow on all he sees.

He stalks the region, starved, at home,
a home where no-one seems to know him.

He looks in through the gates and doors
and hears the griefs that have their source

in sleepers' gasps through clenched teeth,
though that might be just how they breathe

till the moon's gone (the day now brighter),
who was the sorrel's radiant rider.

GOATS IN THE FIELD

From stubble fields in autumn, you goats
are lights of late allure that float

in mist. You fade as night comes on.
You're lost in whiteness and are gone.

When you bow down to the sun's redness,
the killing stone, in readiness;

when you look at the Burning Bush's flare
below the abandoned thoroughfare;

when a mild breeze through haulm can gash
a gold vermillion out of ash;

when sadness grows, by flames bereft;
when not a drop of cordial's left

as the rowan's bitter, the rosehip dry.

AT HOME

A book and kitten grey
beneath my hand.
Saturday and Sunday
breathe through the land.

Lamp rays look back and show
what the spinners spun.
The Word and purring cat
say work is done.

The seventh night somehow
makes deeper shades.
Not long till Christmas now
for whoever waits.

A MEMORY

Snow fell to calm the meek
and bring the great down hard.
Sparrows came in streaks
to root-trash in the yard,

and where they lit, a crowd
of tiny prints were bossed,
much like a hopeful cloud
of snow on hardened frost.

So many stars in snow
and just one human track.
The bird paths left a glow,
the village fallen back.

Just one track, a child's,
like a branch of withered haw
pressed on the white a while,
then vanished in the thaw.

HAY RICK IN WINTER

Behind dark gates, near that
small house beside the lea,
a rick with a white hat
stands out of the way
like God the Father at
the heart of the Trinity.

It calls in crows, has fed
the buntings rummaging under
hay for the last corn head.
It quietly works wonders
and scatters lovely bread
to the poor, near and yonder.

An ancient ladder holds
it up, a conjuror's staff,
key to another world.
It cuts the fog in half
and blue flowers are unfurled –
a gift out of the chaff.

And when it snows at night,
there is one perfect hour
when the ladder, its rungs white,
up to the cloudy towers
beyond the edge of sight
rises with sweet power.

ADVENT IN STARÁ ŘÍŠE

In the first snows
you see the print
of the last geese.

Down to the floes
the branches bent
from the last of trees.

The sun descends,
too shy by half,
in fearful reds.

The Angel of Advent
in dusk sweeps off
clusters of woods.

TWILIGHT

It goes dark on the earth.
Despair is long.
The swan though nearing death
has no song.

Joseph, hopeless, eyes
the cistern's throat.
Led to the sacrifice
a black goat.

The bloodied robes. The woe.
Betrayed existence.
The father grieves. An echo.
Cloud and distance.

JOB IN WINTER

Done shedding leaves,
the trees are bare.
The garden grieves,
arms in the air.

Over rocks and tors
the snow has swarmed.
I shake. These sores
burn with no warmth.

A shroud of snow
for the poor, the ill,
that wraps their limbs
in more cold still.

The farmyard squints
in dark, in fear.
A set of prints
lead to manure.

Flakes fall by
oh so gently.
Around the sky
prints lead to me.

A DEAD CAT

By misery deformed
and washed up here,
a small cat lies.
When quick and spry,
she shared her warmth.

She's waiting still
for a drop of milk
from the snow and moon.
Saturday folds.
Sunday commenced.
The cat against
the moonlight, cold.

Whose guilt is cleansed?

BUT STILL THE LEVINS

To leave at dusk for distant lands
with promises to keep.
Can one return as levins cross
in blood and forests deep,

before nightfall, with autumn near,
the last flames in the west?
To kiss with tenderness and fear
the winter's timid breast.

QUINCE ON THE TABLE

A single wand
of rusted quince,
furred red-blonde,
wonder of scents.

Forehead fragrant.
A cordial kiss.
Perfume flagrant –
the heart feels this.

Warmth of a palm
beyond all scents,
a downy haulm
the sun extends.

The bees and wax
gave us this fruit.
Our lips though cracked
it won't bedew.

Hard fruit to bite.
A foodless feast.
A bitter spite
slowly released.

A magic stone
among the thorns.
Wise virgins' own
pale green lanterns.

A hand pours
oil to the lees.
A nape flares,
as do knees.

The oil now cool.
The fire burns white.
Kindly and tall
they go with lights.

WET SNOW

If this is heavy snow
or rain you cannot know.

Behold the house of the dead.
Behold each drenchèd bed.

Like a face approaching death,
the windows filmed with sweat.

The white veil suffocates
and obstinately waits.

Pools of dark hounds – their prey
a swirling white and gray.

Waters, snow drifts, wind
at play, they twist and sprint.

Snow hunts shades in mid-air
as the hound the hare.

The tracks and the footprints
erased with each new rinse,

relieved at last to drown,
their durance trampled down.

A track in mud, a hangman's
knot. Whose legs will dance?

Snow. Thaw. The water warmed
for Pilate's hands.

SWALLOW

A swallow splayed upon the wall,
black cross in golden radiance, all
round rainbowed with the dew and splayed.
Christ is on the other side,
white and purple, hidden away,
and cooling now; or you could say
it is the swallow's breast itself,
and Christ between the wall and cross
is folded in the shadow lee.
But wait, observe how suddenly
the cross is colored like the veil
that hid the Virgin whom we hail
The swallows mold the bats of mud
upon the wall; the thorns they put
in Christ's brow make it bleed.
From this mud, this Ephphatha,
blossoming like new fire, so fleet
and silent, fire that burns at home,
white and purple, dark as loam,
the swallow his nest shapes and copes
to please Tobiases and Jobs.

AT HOME

A house that has no blinds or gates.
A house that's rarely locked and shuttered.
The long dead live beneath its slates
and meet the pilgrim in the shadows,

returned the old and long way round,
after his searching and wandering.
Breezes wander. Birds are bound
for old nests, circling, wondering.

The night at home. No moon, no stars,
but all the same a brightening ray –
a flame behind the stove-grate's bars
that warms us all here straightaway.

None speaks. When a new shadow streams
into this house, we only gaze.
The native wall's alive, it seems,
beneath these smiles that flare and blaze.

How many pictures hung on it,
how many mirrors, how many shades?
What wounds of nails, the work now quit.
The wall, once clear, so quickly fades.

They died, these doubly asleep.
And then they woke in double force.
And from the ark upon the deep
these outliers sent a raven forth.

And after that a dove. Will it
bring in its mouth an olive leaf?
Could that grow in the flooded silt?
When will the log catch fire and weave

flames on this wall, fling them about?
The ashes play with changing light –
an age of waiting, a branch held out,
the one from which the birds took flight.

They've flown. And in the house, once dim,
a chill resplendence radiates.
Our works and days return, a grim
world full of skeletons and wraiths.

FROST

The hills and mountains bare.
Snow burning.
Like fitches' flash up there
stars twisting, turning.

The shades cling to the house,
They grieve. And through
the garden, drills, and boughs
like lips go blue.

A clear and icy night,
Three Kings by name.
Now read, amazed, who might,
the words in flame.

RUE L...

Now daylight isn't far.
The street is misted silk.
Lead by no morning star
the children go for milk.

Heedless of Paradise,
they yet stand on its threshold.
From window panes they prise
each one a coin of gold.

These lights in children's hands
along the street unfurl,
and the surrounding lands
fade to the underworld.

And on the panes two obols
left for us to take down,
here in this vale of cobbles,
here in the misted dawn.

We'll take them on long roads,
entranced, across the lea,
round waters and through woods,
whispering: *lait*, Lethe...

DOOR

Here is the door, and here
the threshold curved with wear,
the handle, lock, and key.
The pilgrim – where is he?
At last, is hope now near?

The peas sprout in the room.
For each one hours of waiting –
the woes like grain in ground.
And do the tendrils, meeting,
wreathe the doorway round?

Fridays, Sundays: peas
to try the pilgrims' knees.
Their spoons empty and bright.
Who knows are they contrite?

Their broken arms, though colder,
can melt the handle's hoar
with hope, the slightest smolder.
Pea-fragrance at the door...

These wraiths wreathe their way round
the doorway here spellbound.
The handle still ice-cold.
The waiting on the threshold.
With rust, the key is burnt
the lax dead left unturned.

THROUGH THE DARK

If you walk through the dark
you lift a hand to lead.
A hidden branch or bark
will make your temple bleed.

Whose shade goes with us, hands
wounding its dark form? The tracks
bring us to unknown lands,
a coin is paid in tax.

The tree does not step back
and it gives out no light.
The tree's a fish, is black
and netted in the night.

The tree in shadows.
The earth is bare.
The moon and guilt: can those
make our mouths flare?

And will a silent flame
speak from the moon?
And, at that, will guilt name
what makes stones sigh?

PATHS OF HOME

There are paths of stones, of flowers – so far
they then return. Where are we going?
There are eyes that darkness leaves unknowing.
They were and weren't. And here we are.

What are the last words we wait for?

There are paths of rosehip, paths of haws,
the cheating eyes and teeth and claws,
that threaten and that lead our hopes
astray, a mare all bone that slopes
towards swathes for oats and finds old straws.

Gaps in the earth – adders' holes.
Filled with gravel to ease our fears.
The agèd stone of agèd walls
is hammered through long years, long years.

There's hunger. From the tracks it eyes
what was and what is now again.
And sometimes, suddenly, there cries
from where grey roofs meet with grey skies
the firecat Hope in answer, then.
Known of old, it rusts, it blazes;
through children's long-gone eyes it gazes.

Who brushed the wall with burning phrases?

Threaded through its cracks a line
that is a signature and sign.

The wall is windowed. Leaning in
are furrowed brows the stone embosses;
our poverty printed in exhaustion.

Here is some script. After these losses.
A shaky signature: three crosses.

NOVEMBER

A beggar's at the fence.
Uninvited. Invited.
To clothe his nakedness
a line of sticks provided.

Behind the fence of ribs
the heart's unsure, and shy too.
'Take nothing on such trips.
They'll give, if they invite you.'

Pictures in cloud-floes.
A darkened door unheeded.
We are hungry. That goes.
Fear enters, left ungreeted.

Leaf rain. *Rorate cœli*.
A tree. Shades moving greyly.
A fence. The birds were singing.
A rain of blows, woods ringing...

Through stalks, along the glebe,
the hares, rust-colored, creep;
their black eyes in the wold.
Beyond the fence it's cold.
Death wants some warmth to keep.

Naked. Frosty wind.
'This snow and blood I won't
wipe clean – it clothes and warms.'
Mange on skin in swarms.

The starved mouth twists with dread.
Manna of stars outspread.
A pillar of milk, some bread.

A smile? Death laughs instead.

WINDOWS ON STREETS

Picture after picture staying put,
pressed into walls, quicklime and soot.
There are two windows and one door –
a triptych empty, each a drawer
with pledges. Windows in a row.

Uncoiling out for good their glow.

The jugs and loaves of bread the same.
Death sentences glide to a name.

The panes are dark throughout the day.
When parsimony's hair goes grey
and drops its head down in the gloaming
ungladly, but then gladly groaning
– is this tomorrow or yesterday? –
on stony knees, then rising from
the paving's tiles at twilight come
these finished fish of hope, of yearning.
These are the gifts of light, upturning.
Their many scales: coins from a cask
that send their glitter through the dusk.

Such sleights the dark pulls off. So what

then is the light, and what is not?
The opals of each dead fish scale
made pledges, promises, but they failed.

In darkness, opened casement frames.
The needy whisper, have no names.
A curtain's edge, a woman's form,
pleated shadows, linen flames,
an elbow bare, a faded arm.

Promises of glass. The fret
that gutters with a cigarette.
The sparks of greyish-colored wine.
One spark catches, then next door
one's pinched out at the candle's core.
one pinches out the candle-shine.

Sometimes one. Or more. Some guests.

The growths of death, the breasts.

GOOSE IN MIST

It neither burns nor gives a warning.
A goose is calling out this morning.

Behind the wall, lamenting fate,
thus it opens winter's gate.

The doorpost creaks in solitude.
The white door-handle shifts the mood,

from hope to hope, and unsubdued,

the calling wakes the empty yard
to judgment, and the russet orchard.

It also calls the stones and knees
that take in solitude their ease.

Goose: so ashen white its shade,
its wings of mist, so wildly splayed.

Death is warming its white blade.
A sickle sharpened to dark rhythm.

They go. They take nothing with them.

The wall. And trees. Foreheads smashed
against their wall. Blood is splashed.

Behind this wall a mystery.
The blood a trickle. A blackened tree.

SAINT MARTIN

Snow on the fence. Snow on the cape.
Ice in the hair and on the skin,
on hope, on the bare body's shape,
across the fields, the days' chagrin.

Snow falls on human hunger, spreads
on stones as cold as burnt-out coals;
falls on this dog's unbarking head,
on sparrows perched on odd bean-poles.

He promised clouds and they came quick:
snow has no heat – it only clothes.
Night-time. Hope lost in its dark nick.
But hope, a scent, comes when it snows.

Half the cape. Hangs where it falls.
On trellises of ribs. On bone.
On joys stowed in the ground, in walls.
Half the cape. Find joy. One's own.

In white, a finger writes vague tidings
of paradise along the roofs.
And on the cape, consoled, subsiding,
the beggars fall down in their droves.

STICKS IN A FENCE

The fence's sticks, like strings subdued,
forlorn, tacked in a row.
There's much you know of solitude.
Of wings, what do you know?

The straws of wheat don't miss the ears
that heard and were heard too.
You're faceless. Unastonished. Fears –
this lattermath chilled through.

These lean, long years your bony shanks,
waiting, locked in leas.
Burls in palms, heels in mud-banks.
You don't have any knees.

LOOKING FORWARD

We look forward to Saturday,
the garden, friends arriving, greetings.
But all those fences in the way,
those bolts and bars, the latches cheating
fingers, our palms outstretched and bleeding.

And Sunday we look forward to.
But walls and walls won't let us through.
We pound them till we're black and blue.

It's been so long since I've seen you.

Fences lined out like rib-bone.
Glass with crosses overgrown,
with thorns, with spikes, and with chains.

And promises scowl in the panes.

The walls keep growing. Darkness spreads.
The stars light up – teeth of the dead –
light up in gold. Why, and for whom?

We turn back. Alone. Towards home.

CHRISTMAS, 1970

Advent. The Sunday last of all.
Angels, wakening, start to call.

They say: Now rise with us. Now rise.
From forests, fields and from the sties.

We come. We carry nothing. Hands
reach for the manger scene that stands

and waits. It neither chills nor warms
our hopeful, empty, open arms.

It neither chills nor burns. We bring
nothing. And we take nothing.

But someone somewhere calls us now.
A star in clouds? A stone below?

The hand is empty. Thoughts that raced
go still, by the Christ Child embraced.

THE ANGEL OF DISTRESS

With hands of fire and woe
beyond the towers and trees,
he strikes the final blow
on graves like roughened keys,
on bones like strings, oh yes,
he strikes, destroys all ease,
the Angel of Distress,

so these can put on clothes
for Sunday, and from rows
of mud come clambering –
drowsy, tottering,
their shrouds with wormy holes,

deaf and without souls,
withered, lost. They groan
and cry distress from stone,
with teeth, without. For sight,
the eyes are only white.

SWALLOWS FLOWN

The swallows take to their flight-path,
dark brands of mist and aftermath,
black flames, each arrowed like an awl.
Beneath the roof, above the lane,
with soaking reeds they spell a plain
"Amen" in blood across the wall.

They perish, summer's eyes, in pain.

These forget, but I recall.

Escaped. They've left for others' skies,
nails driven in Tobias' eyes,
straws from nests, shards from mud,
desire in shadow-nets for good.

The fish flits deep – a cure that's sought.
Dark's in the net; the fish is not.

They've flown away. In fields, the ricks
have turned to gold; in byres, the bedding.
Esau blesses this by spreading
hay in handfuls. Cow horns nodding
like question-marks on foreheads, tricks
of crooked daggers in the shed,
like scarred half-moons, like the farmstead

lamps put out. Or, rather, not just yet.

Stiff-angled horns about the place
take no-one in their sharp embrace.
Inquiringly they lift a face.

These glows of whiteness sunken down.
By morning, promises gone cold
in hay, the soul beset, run-down.

Left speechless by the dripping lintels,
the columns with their milk-white mantels,
the columns draped with insect mold.

The columns of trees. That bloomed in heaven.
They wait, till winter starts to leaven.

They wait, turned stone beneath the slate.
They wait. For angels now they wait.

MATCH IN A PUDDLE

One black half, one half white.
A fly's barque and its pyre.
The match a soul on fire.
Gone out now, it might

have taken hours, thus drowned
among the guilty shadows.
When? And whose? Who knows?
Maybe homeward bound.

Black foam, and foam that's white,
a pang that poppies hone.
A feather. Its bird has flown
just where? Match thrown aside –

the Reaper's one small bone.

GRAPHIC ART

Still Life with Artist, 1954,
monotype drypoint

Escape to Egypt IV, late 1940s,
drypoint

Depictions of the flight to Egypt and the birth of Christ are situated
in the area of Reynek's home on more than one occasion in his early
graphic work of the late 1940s. He sent these small pictures to his
friends as Christmas and New Year's wishes. This tableau has smooth
and careful cross-hatching, and we see that he has still not completely
mastered drypoint technique. Its naïve stylization attempts to capture
the nocturnal atmosphere of the flight of the Holy Family from
Herod's soldiers.

Calvary II, 1940s,
monotype drypoint

Just before the beginning of World War II, Reynek broached New Testament themes in his graphic art, connecting these with the farmstead in Petrkov and its environs. The most important group is the Passion series (1941–49), to which this early Calvary scene belongs (originally an uncolored monotype). It shows the phastasmic apocalyptic horse-rider, piercing Christ's side with a spear (instead of Longinus the centurion), as the pallid hands of the dead push up between the instruments of Christ's death from the open grave. Reynek took this black apocalyptic figure from Revelations (6.1–8), where four riders presage the end of the world, as well as the suffering that God will visit upon humanity at that time.

Christ on the Door, 1965,
monotype drypoint

Reynek produced about fifty pictures of the Savior on the cross, the crucifixion, and Calvary, employing specific iconographic elements to intensify their expressiveness. In "Crucifixion on Steam Cooker" (1967), Christ's hands are spread out on an apparatus that his son Jiří, who worked in the local agricultural collective, used to prepare food for pigs; elsewhere Reynek's Crucifixions use the door to the byres, across the yard, that had a cat-flap carved out at Christ's legs, and above his head two circular openings, which he used to replace the sun on Christ's right and the moon on his left, as medieval representations depicted it.

Crucifixion VI, 1964,
monotype drypoint

Still legible in this otherwise untraditional Calvary scene are the wheels
of both the eclipsed sun and the moon above Christ, his arms spread
out on the cross, traditional skulls at the foot of the cross as signs
of Adam's original sin and of human mortality, and also the crucified
thieves on either side. The picture has strong, abstract lines and
a diffuse light which creates a dimmed atmosphere. (Such themes were
still unacceptable to communist authorities in Czechoslovakia during
the 1960s.) To the quiet village of Petrkov this brought the members
of the younger generation, who had just, to their astonishment,
discovered the seventy-year old artist.

Ecce Homo, 1949,
monotype drypoint

Reynek depicted this scene, which has had a place in the European tradition since before the Renaissance, with conventional iconographic elements – the crown of thorns and the rushes (a favorite image). But from the late 1940s and even more strongly in the '50s, he rooted Biblical themes in his own domestic environment, in this case the pond at the foot of the slope below the Petrkov farmstead. Here we should note – and this holds for all Reynek's graphic work – that it wasn't the artist's habit to execute his graphic art from careful sketches; rather whenever an idea struck, he would merely draught a few quick lines and then later engrave the scene directly onto the plate.

Ecce Homo II, 1966,
monotype drypoint

After an early treatment of the theme at the end of the 1940s, Reynek returned to the motif of *ecce homo* again toward the end of his life. Thanks to the political thaw in the 1960s this picture appeared in some of Reynek's first exhibitions in Prague and other towns. Here Reynek makes no reference to his own difficult situation, as he would in the somewhat later "Ecce Homo with Moon" (1969), and as he did in his work from the 1940s and '50s, in the Job series. There is a hint of his Petrkov home in the window with a grille and the rough wall printed with Christ's hands. Although this image is stylized and tends toward abstraction (characteristic of Reynek's late period), it includes the crown of thorns above the bloody face of the Savior and the stem of reed, emphasized by the monotype coloring. Also, Reynek adds a red apple to the blood-stained palm, an element not found in traditional iconography.

Pietà at Well, 1949,
monotype drypoint

Reynek's primitive, rustic Romanesque manner allowed him to
escape from the academic mode of the nineteenth century; in the
late 1940s and '50s the style also allowed him to accommodate holy
figures, increasingly against the background of his native Petrkov,
especially the farmstead itself and its garden. This *pietà* is an example,
where the Virgin Mary washes Christ's bloody legs in the flow of
water from a pump, the same one that stood to the side of the main
gate in Petrkov. This relatively early drypoint is executed with great
smootheness and delicacy, where monotype yellow and red colorings
are sparingly used for the golden halo and Christ's bloody wound. Both
tones blend in the evening's redness.

Pietà with Rats, 1966,
monotype drypoint

Seventeen years separate this *pietà* from the preceding one, thus allowing us to see how Reynek matured. On the roughly primed surface of the plate, the raw interior is steeped in twilight. There is a dark opening to a chimney mouth with a dislocated flue, and from below on the right rats attack Christ's helpless body. Martin C. Putna remarked that Reynek's poetic imagination provokes "expressive shock." Jesus and Mary are all the more expressive for the way they are figured with spare lines and in places limned in mere outline.

Pietà with Train Stop, 1968,
monotype drypoint

Reynek returned to the Passion theme of the *pietà* on over twenty
occasions, and his depiction of this image of the holy figures had
become increasingly abstract. The background is, however, clear: in this,
his penultimate *pietà*, he places the scene in front of the rail track with
the local train arriving at the Petrkov stop, with glowing autumnal trees
in the background.

St Veronica I, 1940s,
monotype drypoint

Like his "Calvary II," Reynek particularly liked this early drypoint
with the motif of St Veronica, and so in later prints he applied
a light monotype coloring. The picture is distinctive for the way that
Veronica's arms are spread wide, holding up to our eyes the veil with
the print of Christ's face. Above we see the face of the crucified Christ,
the protruding beams of the cross, and a stylized sun and moon.

Veronica with Spiderweb, 1966,
monotype drypoint

This picture is a good example of the paths that Reynek's inspiration sometimes took, and of the elements that underwrote his iconography. Stylistically related to other works of his mature period of the mid-1960s, "Veronica with Spiderweb" faithfully imitates elements of his Petrkov home with its glass-panelled doors on the ground floor, behind which one can see a further door opening onto the garden. The web woven by the accentuated spider substitutes the traditional veil of Veronica with the print of Christ's face. It prevents her from entering the green paradise, so loved by the artist. The picture reminds us of the long period when Reynek would not enter his own garden, so appalled was he by its devastation at the hands of the tenants billeted there by the socialist authorities.

St Francis with Dove, 1965,
monotype drypoint

Reynek had a great devotion to St. Francis because of his deep affinity
with animals. We also encounter the saint in Francis Jammes's poetic
prose work, *Le Roman du lièvre* (1903), which Reynek translated in 1920
and which was published by Dobré dílo publishers, under Josef Florian.
However, Reynek did not depict the saint in his art until the 1960s,
when this picture was one of his first to be publicly exhibited as a color
print. Georg Stix used it as the main image on the cover of the catalog
for the exhibition at L'Agostiniana gallery in Rome in 1967. Reynek,
ready to experiment, made this engraving of St Francis not in copper
but a less usual material – formica. The hard and unresponsive surface
of the plate stimulated the uncompomising lines of this drypoint.

From the Job cycle, published 1949,
drypoint

Taken from the penultimate series, Job (1949), this picture, like several others in it, reflects not only elements of the artist's Petrkov, but also a kind of metaphorical comparison of Reynek's trying situation during the 1950s with the Old Testament figure from the Land of Uz, who, according to the Book of Job, endured terrible calamities as a result of God's conflict with Satan. Job's herds were displaced, his house was blown away by the wind, and he himself, as the picture attests, was afflicted with terrible, excruciating illnesses. Notwithstanding these travails, Job remained faithful to God, and the series elsewhere shows the face of God, gazing at the peaceful herd.

Return, from the cycle *Don Quixote*, 1955–60,
drypoint

After the difficult years reflected in the Job series, the fourteen-part
series Don Quixote is more in the spirit of the comic hero and marks
a kind of reconciliation, if slightly sarcastic, with the conditions of his
life. In his choice of different situations inspired by Cervantes' work, we
see even more closely the outlines of Reynek's home. Such is the case of
"Return," which has a winter mood and shows the artist's farmstead in
the background.

Stairs, 1963,
drypoint

Reynek engraved several self-portraits and portraits of his children, but the genre did not not suit him and they have a limited emotional range. Exceptions to this are those of his later years where Reynek gave up on realistic figuration, gaining access to deeper forms of interiority. This holds both for "Still Life with Painter" (1954) and "Stairs" from the high point of the 1960s, which brings Reynek's art to a close. The artist, in straightforward silhouette with a basket for wood, goes up the stairs to the window, beneath which the steps turn to the next floor.

Yard in Winter II, 1955,
monotype drypoint

Winter was the season that brought the farmstead at Petrkov into its own, and the snow-covered yard, with its gate open to the village, is characteristic. It is executed effectively, the upper reaches thriftily colored with monotype. The cow being led off adds a dimension to this genre scene (even though the Reyneks' actual cow had been taken by the state several years earlier).

Closing the Byre, 1962,
monotype drypoint

Winter again, with footprints in the snow. Reynek pays close attention
to these later and in some pictures, with both nature and Biblical
themes, the prints are an important motif which mark the birth and
passing of the creatures that made them. They thaw and fade, as
faithfully suggested by even this small tableau.

Pastoral X, from the cycle *Pastoral*, published 1947,
drypoint

The series Snow depicted Reynek's area of the Czech-Moravian
Highlands during the winter; at this time pastoral themes were also
important. One reason was that sheep gradually became part of the
the artist's life. "So that I can avoid encountering people, I have
a herd of sheep that I recently bought. They bring them here from the
bombed regions in the north. I'm glad that it worked out," Reynek
writes to a friend in 1941. The result was a twelve-part series, engraved
in the years 1942–1945 and published by Vlastimil Vokolek in Pardubice
in 1947.

Goat by Road, 1964,
monotype drypoint

Reynek did not invent the scenes and situations of his graphic art – he was faithful in his depictions of the landscape, the animals, and people. Here a small goat turns his face to us dramatically, standing beside the foot-stones along the road, curving from the artist's Petrkov to the neighboring village of Lípa.

Turkey II, 1965,
monotype drypoint

The animals and birds in Reynek's yard are not those of a biology
textbook. Here they move through oneiric space, with an
inconspicuous ladder at the side, another significant element which has
more than a decorative function, as its rungs lead heavenward.

Cat on Wall II, 1957,
drypoint

Cats were an integral part of Reynek's life and art, and here's one
with a wall and other objects scattered through the dry grass in windy
weather. We find the cat everywhere in pictures both sacred and
profane, its unpeaceful, wandering soul sanctifying whatever space it
entered.

November, 1967,
monotype drypoint

Reynek would impress even the smallest plates with extraordinary poetic force, catching the moods that wended through him. Two small figures, somewhere near the gate of the farmstead, beneath the bare trees, are immersed in the twilight. At their feet is a covey of geese, incandescent in the gloom. He took much care and time with the latter, scratching off all the color to intensify the contrast.

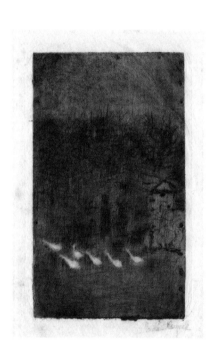

Summer's End, 1958,
monotype drypoint

Like the previous picture, this is set in a particular time; but here the
mood is pervaded with melancholy, concentrated in the tree with
maturing fruit, on which a pair of pheasants alight, with haystacks in
the background emerging from fog. There are perhaps memories of
Reynek's years as a student in Jihlava; but this also catches the period in
which he wrote the collection, *Fall's Butterflies*, the postwar collection
in which he definitively parted with his youth and faced equably into
old age.

Road in Winter, 1960,
hand-colored drypoint

Smaller figures play a role in Reynek's work, and are not the product of fantasy. He chose particular figures from Petrkov, which he knew well, and honors them in his pictures.

FOUR POEMS BY SUZANNE RENAUD

Translated by David Wheatley

HARVEST MOON

Scarlet as the sea was once
tonight the unco moon swept by,
lording it over from us from on high:
an eerie Potter's Field with doors
thrown open on the raging fires
that lick and leap from Hell's far ends.

TOM THUMB

Night falls, and what remains?
Three pebbles, three millet grains.

Dark night falls and with it doubts
covering over all our routes.

But also in the woods a spark
that signals to us through the dark.

And among the shades a sigh
asking of us: reply, reply...

WEARISH OLD TREE

Wearish old tree the last rays of the sun
have bathed gently in their solemn light:
burning bush, abandoning tonight
the earth you always lay so barely on...

Tragic and denuded Marie Celeste
of the teeming dark and the fog and wind
on riverbanks in evening shade, but bound
elsewhere, swept on in search of kingdoms lost.

Still for now your scarlet mantle billows
over the heart that scents our coming loss
impassively... and all our noisy cares
are birds lingering in terminal bliss
in your cage of light with its fine gold bars.

DAY OF THE DEAD, 1938

We blow about like the north wind
crazed with nostalgia for the light.
Revolt gives way to prayer too late
for the remorse that gnaws the mind
now that we've become the north wind
and rainfall on stones at night.

Ah, the look of eternal rest
cast so palely over our ruin...
the faces and the dates strewn
over the book of death crossed
by blind shadows and the moon.

Blown wherever the north wind blows
in what poor potholed skies
have we not been doomed to whine
begging you, light, to hear our cries
and grant us a death to call our own?

ESSAYS ON BOHUSLAV REYNEK

BOHUSLAV REYNEK: FROM CATHOLIC COUNTERCULTURE AND THE APOCALYPSE TO A HIGHLAND FARM

The idea of Catholic literature provokes mixed reactions. Readers will perhaps be reminded of devotional literature, turned in toward the church and its circles, even as it polemicizes sharply with the modern world. This is often accurate: Catholic literature as a distinct phenomenon does not emerge until the modern secular period, when Catholics were in the minority – that is, in Western Europe in the nineteenth century, in Central and Southern Europe for the most part not until the twentieth century. Reacting to secularization, Catholicism creates its own special social milieu, its own culture, and also its own literature. Generally, this last is not aesthetic in its ambitions, rather it serves as a kind of communal defence.[1] Paradoxically, inside this culture extraordinary artistic works occasionally emerge that find a wider contemporary readership. Sometimes they find even greater recognition outside than inside the church milieu.

Why is this? Certainly, in the first instance, it is because outstanding artistic talents can emerge anywhere, regardless of religious or political conviction. But Catholicism brings with it certain assumptions that foster talents of a particular kind. Or, in other words, while it is true that Catholic culture's stance toward the modern world is negative, it responds to it polemically; it is, properly speaking, reactionary. But this reaction, this hostility that provokes Catholic artists to pitch themselves against the modern world, can find expression in exceptional works of art. Catholic

---

[1] See Martin C. Putna, *Česká katolická literatura v evropském kontextu 1848-1918* [The European Context of Czech Catholic Literature, 1848–1918] (Prague: Torst, 1998), and Martin C. Putna, *Česká katolická literatura v kontextech 1918-1945* [The Contexts of Czech Catholic Literature, 1918–1945] (Prague: Torst, 2010). Of the studies that map the developments of Catholic literature in Europe and their effects on Czech culture, the following are available in English (or at least partly in summaries): Martin C. Putna "Searching for a 'Fourth Path': Czech Catholicism between Liberalism, Communism, and Nazism," in *Christianity and Modernity in Eastern Europe*, ed. Bruce R. Berglund and Brian Porter-Szucz (Budapest: Central European University Press, 2010), 85–109; and Martin C. Putna, "European Catholic Literature, and the Reception accorded to Canon Sheehan in Czechia," in *Revisiting Canon Sheehan of Doneraile (1852–1913): Author, Activist, Priest*, ed. Gabriel Doherty (Wells: Smenos Publications, 2014), 82–90.

culture, in some of its forms, takes on the lineaments of counterculture, to use the term of the anthropologist Theodore Roszak.

In his foundational work, *The Making of a Counter Culture* (1969), Roszak focuses on the left-wing youth movements of his time (it is subtitled *Reflections on the Technocratic Society and Its Youthful Opposition*). He uses the early Christians in the Roman Empire as a historical analogy, discussing how they built a parallel world during the period when, up to the reign of Constantine, they were outlaws. In Roszak's description, youth counterculture, like the culture of the early Christians and other countercultures in history, is founded on the anticipation of a great turn, whether it is violent revolution, peaceful revolution, the return of a golden age for humanity, God's Kingdom, the Apocalypse, or a vast conflagration. This radical, countercultural, eschatological, apocalyptic disposition is found in the artists of modern Catholicism. From such a position remarkable works can emerge. This is precisely the case of the *oeuvre* of Bohuslav Reynek (1892–1971).

The roots of Reynek's spiritual formation are in France. Throughout the nineteenth century and in the first half of the twentieth, France was the center of Catholic literature in Europe. Classic works by François-René de Chateaubriand, Ernest Hello, Paul Claudel, Jacques Maritain, and Georges Bernanos created the model stances, characteristic genres, and aesthetic judgements that were adopted and transformed by Catholic communities in other European countries: from Ireland to Austria, Slovenia, Portugal, Lithuania, and in the lands that would become Czechoslovakia in 1918. England, similar in many respects, but distinct in others, with influential and authoritative figures such as John Henry Newman, R. H. Benson, G. K. Chesterton, and later Evelyn Waugh and Graham Greene, was a special case. For Czech Catholic culture the dominant influence was the French model, and this was especially true for the very particular group in which Reynek found himself.

This was the community of Stará Říše, which took its name from a village in the Czech-Moravian Highlands (by felicitous chance the place name means Ancient Realm). It was founded by Josef Florian (1873–1941), a publisher and translator by profession. In cultural terms, Stará Říše was simply a publishing house that won early renown for its revelatory translations of Medieval mysticism and modern Expressionist poetry, as well as for its high production and design standards (the books are now collector's items). But these publishing and translating activities were only the outer sign of an inner program, which was apocalyptic. Josef Florian believed that the end of world was approaching, as predicted by the apparition of the Virgin Mary in the French Alpine village of La Salette in 1846, a conviction promulgated by the French writer Léon Bloy (1846–1917) in novels of dark romanticism and grotesquely polemical pamphlets. Bloy's books about the apparition at La Salette and other prophesies were the original core of Florian's publishing. Moreover, Florian formed his own conviction – which for the most part he promulgated in informal talks – that his community was chosen to protect iniquitous Europe from the approaching flood of fire. Thus, his publication of beautiful books: not for culture's sake itself, but because the Stará Říše community would salvage a core artistic heritage for spiritual ends. Once the necessary books were ready, they would leave together for Ethiopia, which was to be the single country left untouched for uncorrupted Christians. With the passing of the years and with the further publication of beautiful books, the apocalyptic fervor of the community waned, while the publishing house continued its work.

Put in such a bare manner, this would seem to be merely an obscure apocalyptic sect, but in its time it was enormously attractive for many radically minded young men. In the same way that many converted to communism during the period, so others converted to Florian's radical Catholicism. That these two diametrically opposed positions had much in common is confirmed by the fact that some of Florian's converts were previously young communists; and that Florian's Catholicism placed a strong emphasis on social justice (his astringent critique of a bourgeois, capitalist, selfish, and pitiless world certainly equaled that of Communists). Of the leading figures of Czech Catholic culture in the first half of the twentieth century, practically all had either direct contact with Stará Říše (staying there on occasion), personally encountered Florian (an almost Socratic figure who himself wrote next to nothing), or were influenced by Florian's books. The radical, extremist style – oscillating between exaltation and the grotesque – which Florian, following Léon Bloy, made his own, became canonical for many modern classic authors of Czech Catholic literature. Bohuslav Reynek was among the young men upon whom Josef Florian had a colossal influence. Although he never lived in Stará Říše and was too far away to be a neighbor, he was near enough for there to be regular contact. Reynek spent most of his life on the family farmstead (originally a small château) in the village of Petrkov, also in the Czech-Moravian Highlands. Not quite neighbors, this created the conditions for an extensive correspondence between Reynek and Florian. His influence, in Reynek's case, took a striking turn, as Reynek's *oeuvre* is appealing not only for ordinary Catholic readers, but also for those who occupy the faith's radical and apocalyptic fringes.

Reynek's earliest works are influenced by the Czech symbolism and decadence of the time. However, the poems from 1914 forward are marked by the fateful meeting and his conversion (or reconversion) experience under Florian's influence. With his whole being Reynek accepted this faith inflected so deeply by Bloy, La Salette, and Florian, and this became the main theme and expressive means of his poetry.

His central preoccupation is the repeated celebration of a truth that can be summed up thus: the world, sunk in evil and suffering, awaits the flood of God's fire. The imminence of the apocalypse and the salvation of the world was prophesied by the Virgin Mary, Our Lady of Dolors. For Reynek, this teaching was not the stuff of literature, but a description of the coming reality, as we can see from his correspondence with Florian and other members of the community. In 1914, when this correspondence began, Reynek wrote enthusiastically about his reading of Léon Bloy, adopting from Bloy and Florian the same exalted style and the same desire to find prophesies that would confirm the approaching flood of fire and the end of the world: "Perhaps we will live to see the new glory of France! I often think that the real converts of today, of which there are enough in France, such as Claudel, Jammes, Péguy, and others, are a kind of foreshadowing of the turning of that entire land. Perhaps the present punishment will awake it and allow the blind to see."[2] Only during the 1920s does this apocalyptic fervor abate, and the letters to Stará Říše begin to be devoted instead to art and poetry.

---

[2] Letter to A. L. Stříž, 3 September 1914, in *Bohuslav Reynek: Korespondence* [Bohuslav Reynek: Correspondence], ed. Jaroslav Med and Jiří Šerých (Prague: Charles University Press, 2012), 27.

Two of the central motifs of Florian's apocalypticism, the weeping Virgin and the coming fire, along with the motif of waiting, are the dominant elements in the conversion phase of Reynek's work. However, he is no straightforward exponent of the idea of history we find in Bloy, La Salette, and Florian. From their correspondence, we see that Florian desired Reynek's services as a translator, and even more his financial assistance (because of his farmstead, Reynek was markedly better off than most of the community's members), but he did not consider Reynek's own poetry important. In the context of the sect's preparations for the Flood, Reynek's literary endeavors were merely a private activity. Only with the publication of *Lip by Tooth* (1925) did Florian's attitude change. That collection was indeed personal in its contours, but it also displayed an artistic independence, for all Reynek's whole-hearted identification with the sect. He turned the apocalyptic motifs toward his own inner world, connecting the newness of Florian's ideas with older images of church liturgy and iconography. On the one hand, this grounded the new motifs within tradition, and provided expressive means for the new teaching so its message was clear even to those beyond the initiates; on the other hand, the old motifs of Catholicism took on a new significance, a new dynamic. Reynek identifies the apocalyptic Virgin Mary of La Salette with the traditional image of the *pietà*. The iconic *pietà* is also, after all, Our Lady of Sorrows. Christ is unmoving, incapable of action, dead. The sole active agent, though she only weeps, is Mary. To figure the flood of fire Reynek finds a traditional anchoring in the motif of Pentecost, as the Holy Spirit descends in flaming tongues upon the apostles. On the other hand, the most apocalyptic motif – waiting for the great change – is not present in Reynek's early poetry. His waiting is unconnected with established liturgical, theological or iconographic figures.

Reynek finds expressive means for this apocalyptic theme in the line which he used in his translation work: his first book-length translation, Charles Péguy's *La Tapisserie de Sainte Geneviève et de Jeanne d'Arc* (French publication, 1913), was published in 1915, and then in 1920 further poems by Péguy, and Paul Claudel's *Processionnal pour saluer le siècle nouveau* (French publication, 1907) and *Cinq grandes Odes* (French publication, 1911). Both these grandiloquent standard bearers of Catholicism use a similar long line that often runs over several lines of text. It is rhetorical, choric, and sometimes stamped with an end rhyme – a capacious vehicle for the convert who desires to announce his faith to the world. Reynek uses this Péguy-Claudel line for most of the poems of *Thirsts* (written 1912–1916), and the three sections published in Stará Říše's *Nova et Vetera* journal, "Supplication to the Virgin Mary" (1915), and the sequences "Palm Sunday" and "Earth's Grief" (both written 1918). Form and content harmonize perfectly, and these publications are exactly coincident with Reynek's period of conversion. The convert's exaltation, augmented by his new membership in a keenly apocalyptic community, could hardly be sustained. At a certain moment, disillusionment and depression comes. This may have been caused by disappointment after seeing the church up close, or having become familiar with the particular community that surrounded the convert, or after having gazed into the depths of his own soul, or perhaps it was just a natural psychological reaction. In any case, tense anticipation of a total metamorphosis of life and the world cannot be maintained indefinitely. The following post-conversion phase of Reynek's work reveals nothing of the causes. Instead it bears witness to the spiritual drama taking place within, to the ever stronger waves of anxiety, to feelings of weakness and enervation. The poet calls on God to intervene, to manifest himself more strongly, renovating the prior state of unconditional unity.

Reynek arranged these poems of religious anxiety into the cycles "Quiet Moment" and "Journey to Bethlehem," and then joined these with the two sequences published earlier at Stará Říše, "Palm Sunday" and "Earth's Grief," incorporating them into his most extensive collection, which he titled *Earth's Grief* (completed 1921, published 1924). There is sense in this arrangement: the book's first two sequences are those of the fresh convert, the second two emerge from the aftermath of the first exaltation. In the first two, joy prevails; in the second two, anxiety. There are formal parallels: in the first two sequences the Péguy-Claudel line predominates; in the second two, he uses an irregular free-verse line.

Religious commitment not having provided Reynek in his post-conversion state with the kind of fulfillment that he hoped for, he turns with dissatisfaction to another poetic theme and indeed to other expressive means than those of the convert's bliss. Now, Reynek executes two maneuvers, both inspired by his translation work. The *oeuvre* of Francis Jammes, whose *Le Roman du lièvre* (French publication 1903), which Reynek translated (Czech publication 1920), leads him to what at first might seem a banal recognition, but which turns out to be revelatory for him at this juncture: that it is possible to experience and express the religious dimension of the world not only in the repetition and variation of sacred words and sentences, but also through the perception of small, profane, and mundane things and realities – these are witnesses to and participants in invisible mysteries. This changes his imaginative direction. Above all, the section "Quiet Moment" from *Earth's Grief* lowers the poet's gaze from elevated dogmas and signs of the apocalypse – as is clear from titles of poems such as "April Rain," "For the Pigeons in the Lattermath," "For the Apple Trees," "For a Cuckoo," and "For the Wild Thyme." Only by gazing down in this way does the poet experience proximate joy. Nevertheless, the language which conveys this downward gaze is, even with the loosening of the line, high, odic, and effusively descriptive.

The work of the Austrian expressionist Georg Trakl (1887–1914), whose two collections Reynek translated soon after their original publication (*Gedichte* [in German, 1913, in Czech, 1917], *Sebastian im Traum* [likewise 1915, 1924]), leads him elsewhere to develop a general sense of gloom and drastic detail – worms slithering along the ground, dead fish, hair spattered with blood, old wrinkled skin. It also leads him to a tendency to liberate colors from their objects, allowing them equal valency in the poem. Trakl allowed Reynek to express post-conversion disillusionment in refined, aestheticized images of suffering, illness, and decomposition; one important consequence of this was a shift in emphasis to the beauty of poetic language as an end in itself. Moreover, Reynek adopted the genre of the prose poem, which was used by Trakl on occasion in *Sebastian im Traum*. In this mode he wrote *Fish Scales* (1922) and *Snake on the Snow* (1924), and this has led to his being numbered among the Czech exponents of German expressionism. Such a characterization is corroborated by the frontispiece of both books, which were by an artist also considered expressionist, Reynek's friend in correspondence, Josef Čapek. Apocalyptic-liturgical motifs – the Last Judgement, Advent, the *pietà* – are present in these books, but they are handled differently, with the unusual, if sometimes shocking, conjunction of the devout and the cruel, of immediacy and aestheticism, of objects and colors. The centuries-long Catholic cultural heritage provided him with many ways of treating the images of the suffering of Christ and of last things.

In both collections, Reynek's prose poems attend to the small creatures and things of this world, consolidating this downward gaze. However, he now writes of them not so as to sing of their purity and godliness, but to lament and pay homage to their beautiful passing, part of which is their physical decomposition. *Lip by Tooth* is a kind of settling of accounts. It marks the struggle to find both inner balance as well as a poetic canon. The collection demonstrates the importance of the preceding phase of spiritual and religious development, and the new influences. Here these come into conflict for the last time, so that they can be re-forged in a new form – Reynek's major style. For the last time a young man appears as lyric speaker (no longer young any more, in any case, and perhaps this is why he speaks so urgently about his life, particularly about his emotional and erotic anguish). A year after the publication of *Lip by Tooth*, the poet married and began a family. Without wishing to view this fact as somehow causative, we cannot ignore that his establishment in life occurs at the same time that he finds his definitive shape as a poet. The Reynek of the major style now stays beyond the border of his poems, and they are thus more objective than subjective. His own self as a distinct subject, who speaks of what he does and what he feels, is now omitted from the poems.

Post-conversion anxiety is still present in *Lip by Tooth*. Now, however, it is no longer experienced as unendurable torment. On the contrary, it is gradually accepted as a permanent state, residing deep in the spirit, a state which is allotted by God to the poet. In this book, for the first time, the small world of the village regularly appears, any part of which – an animal, tree, signs of the season or time of day – points to God's order and the damaged nature of earthly existence, for instance in "Dawn in Winter," "Idyll, Morning," "Fly in Lamp," "Ducks in the Yard," "Stump in the Fire," and "The Yard in April." This is no straightforward nature description: the eponymous kid goats of one poem lead the poet to remember the blessing of Isaac in the Old Testament (the motif of the goatskin which disguised Jacob); roosters remind us of Peter's denial of Jesus; the willow shoots of Christ arriving on Palm Sunday riding a donkey; the animal young condemned to death, a symbol of all humanity. In contrast with the preceding phases, the latitude of poetic concentration has contracted. We are not yet finally in the Petrkov farmyard, as in the later collections – it is still possible to wander out and return, whether via a distracted memory, or a poetic motif from another country or cultural milieu. However, the narrow way lay clearly ahead.

In the spiritual subsoil of *Lip by Tooth* we can distinguish three motifs of Florian-esque apocalypse from the conversion phase. They have, however, undergone "de-apocalyptization": the iconographic *pietà* remains one of the key images of Reynek's inner landscape, but the doleful Madonna has lost her original connection with the apocalyptic Virgin Mother of La Salette and remains only a traditional symbol of pain, sympathy, and consolation, pertinent to every human life. The Pentecostal motif of the Holy Spirit's flames has almost completely disappeared – the only trace is the redness we find in several poems. This is most striking in the later collection, *Fall's Butterflies* (1946), where redness, in a motif of fire or blood (the burning bush, the crimson heart, fiery longing, etc.) concludes the greater part of the poems. This redness always signifies hope amidst anxiety, and resistance to logic and probability; hope that comes with the "now-it-has-happened" death of Christ, and the "now-it-approaches" death of man. The third apocalyptic motif, that of waiting, has not disappeared, but has changed in nature. Before, he was situated in the early twentieth century, waiting for the end of the world; now it shifts to the humbler level of the individual's salvation. This is also a move from history to metahistory: from the new Apocalypse of Florian back to the older, traditional, and familiar Apocalypse, which the holy days remind the Catholic faithful. Thus Reynek, in his mature and late phases, is drawn rather to All Souls, the Feast of Christ the King, and Advent rather than Pentecost – that is, times and feast days that have an aspect of quiet, humble waiting.

In *Lip by Tooth* Traklesque images of aestheticized ruin and decay still appear. It is as though Reynek wishes, in his celebration of the unaesthetic aspects of some creatures, to provoke expressionistic shock, which we can see in the recurring motifs of the fly and the spider. Reynek's particular expressionism is thus grounded in the country farmyard, where he can find details just as shocking and harrowingly beautiful as those that other expressionists found in modern cities. However, what has changed utterly in his continued employment of Traklesque principles is the poetic line itself which has contracted from broad profusion to straitened concentration. As the physical range of the poet's attention has narrowed and sharpened, so too has the space of the text itself. Up to this, Reynek's poetry had spread outward, enabled in this by the Péguy-Claudel choric line and the prose-poem. Now this contracts, as though Reynek had decided to be sparing with words, intimating that best of all would be to keep silent. Just as Reynek's poetry up to this tried to be one of richness – high, artistic, metaphorical – now it seems that it finds its finest expression in simplicity and lack of ornament.

Reynek did not publish another collection until *The Sowing of Solitude* (1936), and he emerges after a decade filled with joyful family concerns, among these, annual moves between Petrkov and Grenoble (the hometown of his wife, the poet Suzanne Renaud [1889-1964]), and intense work on his drawings and graphic art. He emerges as a poet who has, in a way, returned home to find his true form, with which he will remain to the end. Of course, this does this does not entail absolute stasis – Petrkov is not an ivory tower. In the collection *Pietà*, he calls on Czech saints at a time of national peril ("Wayside Shrine"). The collection *A Frosted Pane* (1969) originated in the first half of the 1950s, the period of greatest humiliation for both the country and Reynek's family, when his farmstead was collectivized, and he and his two sons were then assigned to it by the Communist authorities as day laborers. The horizon of his poetry narrows even further and motifs of silent anxiety are stronger, almost desperate, and these are projected into Biblical images in the poems, "The Torture of Animal Young," "Bloody Sweat," "Akeldama," and "Toward *Dies Irae*." Some tragic motifs in his final collection, *Swallows Flown* (samizdat publication 1978, then officially 1989), are related to the political events of 1968. Nevertheless the fundamental outlines of Reynek's poetry do not change. The major style is comprised of the collections *Pietà* (1940), *Fall's Butterflies*, the group of poems from the 1940s and 1950s, *Snow at the Door*, and *A Frosted Pane*, and the final, posthumously published *Swallows Flown*.

The major style of this poetry stems from *Lip by Tooth*, only it is more pared down and simplified. In formal terms it is perhaps the simplest poetry that has ever been written in Czech. Its core is the same and single concept, discovered in *Lip by Tooth*: animals, objects, the seasons, and times of day, which all point to liturgical and Biblical imagery. This latter in turn leads back to the former. In the correspondences the tormented soul of the poet is lulled, finding a delicate balance – even though that soul does not enter the arena of the poem to describe its experiences. After almost four decades, nothing further, nothing more. From this reduced, simple approach came what many consider to be one of the greatest achievements of Czech poetry.

Literary critics have already analyzed the various aspects and parts of this final form: the nuanced significances of the animal motifs, the parallels between the development of Reynek's visual art and his poetry, the theological idea of sin behind the poet's vision of the world, or epiphany, the manifestation of hidden zones in simple things.[3] It is striking, however, that most of the abovementioned works deal with the phase before the establishment of the major style – that is, when Reynek was still developing and when the poetry was more descriptive in nature. Studies to date thus confirm how difficult it is to engage critically with Reynek's major period, as though the very means to speak of it were lacking, that is, if we wish to avoid merely repeating what has been said before about Petrkov and Grenoble, Florian and Trakl, translation and engraving, poverty and piety, animals and twilights. The exceptional nature of Reynek's achievement, however, can be understood in another way, through comparative poetics; these provide literary concepts or approaches, which illuminate typological similarities, even though there is little genetic connection with Reynek. More particularly, there are three parallels.

---

[3] Respectively, Miroslav Červenka, "Bestiář Bohuslava Reynka" [Bohuslav Reynek's Bestiary], in *Styl a význam* [Style and Significance] (Prague: Československý spisovatel, 1991), 68–88; Dagmar Halasová, *Bohuslav Reynek* (Brno: Petrov, 1992); Jaroslav Med, "Bohuslav Reynek – básník samoty a kontemplace" [Bohuslav Reynek: Poet of Solitude and Contemplation], in *Spisovatelé ve stínu* [Writers in Shadow] (Prague: Zvon, 1995), 101–13, and further studies by the same author; Xavier Galmiche, "Epifanie. Zrození básnického obrazu v díle Bohuslava Reynka" [Epiphany: The Origination of the Poetic Image in the Work of Bohuslav Reynek] in *L'oeuvre de Bohuslav Reynek – Une éclaircie au loin... Essais sur le discours de l'Europe éclatée 2000* (Grenoble: Romarin, 2000), 117–30.

The first parallel is between Reynek and Chinese poetry and art.[4] Critics who approach Reynek primarily as an artist have established this analogy. In her study, *Bohuslav Reynek* (1992), Dagmar Halasová points to the direct influence of Chinese forms – Reynek was familiar with Chinese fine arts and of Czech versions of Chinese poetry (by Bohumil Mathesius). In contrast, those critics who approach Reynek primarily as a writer avoid this parallel – perhaps concerned that the influence is difficult to establish, or that his image as a Catholic poet will be contaminated. Still, the parallel between classical poetry of the Tang Dynasty and Reynek's major style is clear, and is founded on the same minimalism of motif and expression. A few words, freely yet precisely placed beside each other. A few small motifs from the same repertoire. A few small metamorphoses within an archetypal landscape. The parallel goes even deeper than these formal aspects. The likeness has to do with the entire concept of the work of poetry and the poet's personality. The minimalist austerity of Chinese poetry is in reality just as deceptive as the lapidary simplicity of Reynek's major work, as both possess a rich, broad hinterland that is invisible in the text: in Reynek's case, it is the breadth of his own earlier forms and the way he absorbed his influences; in the case of the Chinese poets it is the richness of their study of tradition and poetic codes. These are the reasons why both poetries can, with virtuosic flair, work so well with nuance and intimation: Reynek doesn't describe what happens in church during the liturgy of Advent, Christmas, or All Souls. Rather he curtly gestures toward the symbolism and mood of a particular feast day, often merely by mentioning its name. Similarly, Chinese poetry is full of hidden references to other poems, texts, and traditional motifs, and, like Reynek's, it is not concerned whether readers understand these. If some readers do not understand, then they are uneducated and stand outside the circle of initiates; the fault lies with them.

Moreover, Reynek, in his life and work, though he did not know it, perfectly corresponds with the ideal of a Chinese poet – a man in the

---

[4] See Aleš Roleček, "Samoty čínské, samoty vysočinské" [Chinese Solitudes, Highland Solitudes], in *Hluboká: Kulturní dějiny jednoho skrytého místa* [Hluboká: A Cultural History of a Hidden Place], ed. Štěpán Bartoš, Martin C. Putna, and Aleš Roleček (Prague: Malvern, 2012), 109–14.

margins, a hidden saint, a *yinshi*, or hermit, who has withdrawn from the world to a waste land to live in poverty and Spartan circumstance, a man who only occasionally, at odd moments of his contemplative life, writes a few lines or paints a small, simple landscape in ink. Such apparently useless and private activity has, however, a spiritual dimension: the writing of poetry, the engraving of graphic art, and the pouring of milk for cats has an immeasurable significance for the entire world, since through concealed correlations it helps balance the rancor of life and correct its disturbed balance. Reynek, too, believes in the concealed correlation of all deeds, and that what is manifest is influenced by what is hidden; after all, he was a Catholic schooled in his youth by Léon Bloy and his "cosmic balances of sympathy," which have analogies in Chinese Buddhism and Taoism. The position of this poet-hermit in relation to the world that he has abandoned is ambiguous. On the one hand he is honored and respected, sometimes sought out by pupils and admirers; on the other, he is sometimes mocked as eccentric and mad. For example, the Tang poet Hanshan emphasizes his mad attributes. And in one unpublished poem Reynek breaks with his practice to speak of himself slightingly: "In my village, I'm the fool. / Sad dogs know me." Then, toward the end of his life, Reynek experienced the second aspect of Chinese poet-hermits when an admiring world sought him out in his waste land.

The second parallel is with Russian authors, the poetic celebrants of impoverished aristocratic demesnes. The château of Petrkov is a similar island of the old world, appointed with simple and natural beauty for the sojourn of a simple person, like the dilapidated melancholic estates that are described by Anton Chekhov and Ivan Bunin. The new world, modern and inhuman, is everywhere preparing to invade (and did indeed invade the yard at Petrkov). Chekhov's heroes in *The Cherry Orchard* and Bunin's characters in *Antonov Apples* lack the strength to fight openly with this new world order. Rather they resist it by retaining to the last possible moment pieces of the old world, and all the more intensely experience the narrowed space, and all things and relations in it. Reynek belongs here too: the straitened circumstances of the house at Petrkov provide its inhabitants, joined in adversity, with both the strength to silently resist destruction and the possibility of experiencing even more deeply than before an intimacy with the values of the old world (just as with the smallest things and creatures, so too with the most exalted symbols and names of the Christian faith, as we see in the titles of the pictures "Pietà Beyond the Garden" and "Crucifixion on a Hot Day").

Unlike Russian witnesses of this decline, Reynek does not describe the particular conditions of his life (the house amidst the neglected garden and his difficult struggles with ill-disposed neighbors). These remain unexpressed, the silent context of his lines. However, they make up the invisible background which contributes to its intensity. The Reynek cult, the myth, has thus correctly incorporated the house in Petrkov as integral part of his canonical image. Only with these is our picture of late Reynek's lines and etchings complete. However, given the numerous accounts, photographs, filming, and figuring of what remained hidden, a danger arises, one that his spare artistic creations before the discovery of Petrkov did not face, that is, the danger of creating the idea of a country idyll, the danger, then, of kitsch.

The third parallel returns us to the very beginnings of poetry itself, to the Latin word *carmen*. This word can be translated in three ways – as song, as poem, or as spell (whether magical or religious). In the beginning these three possibilities were one. Then the paths of poetry, music, and magic parted. In the twentieth century it would turn out that poetry was weakest of the three siblings. Those who realized this weakness sought to renovate its strength by once more joining what had been divided, searching for a connection between poetry and music, poetry and magic, poetry and mysticism – as is evident in the work of Henri Bremond.[5] Often they presumed that to achieve such musicality, magicality, or mysticality, poetry had to move *ahead* to new and as yet unheard-of poetic forms. Bohuslav Reynek's work is in contrast a journey backward, a return to that which is simplest and most basic. On the formal level, this means a return to the oldest metrical forms of Czech poetry. Reynek's rhymed tetrameter couplets, ever oscillating between accentual and syllabic, strikingly remind us of the line of Czech medieval lyrics. But the intuitive move toward this line and its few variants is not the main, demonstrable source of Reynek's poetic effect. It is rather an outward sign that Reynek, without consciously attempting it, was able to return to

---

[5] Cf. Henri Bremond, *Prière et poesie* (Paris: Bernard Grasset, 1926).

the very origins of the Czech poetic word – to the primal *carmen*, a poem that affects the reader at once like a song, a spell, and a prayer.

Three parallels – Chinese, Russian, and medieval Czech – help us to understand the character of Reynek's work. At the same time they enable us to understand why, from the 1960s on, a cult grew up around him, and not only in Catholic circles. Poets, painters, photographers, art historians, and even musicians – members of the counterculture and, after the Soviet invasion of 1968, dissidents and members of the underground, all started journeying to Petrkov. Only in these final years of the poet's life did the Reynek myth emerge. This myth is more icon than narrative. More than any other Czech Catholic writer, Reynek is connected with the canonized image of a man of constancy and simplicity. Most frequently we see this in the photographs of Dagmar Hochová, which figure a small, old man, sitting at the stove in an old farm house, either engraving a steel plate, or stroking a cat. The Reynek myth spread in the circles of unofficial culture up to 1989. Toward the regime's end, Reynek became a cult figure for a good part of the emerging generation of poets, who were searching for models outside official literature. After the Velvet Revolution Reynek's story gradually became part of the general canon of stories about twentieth-century Czech culture. The paradoxical stamp of this myth was the enormous exhibition of Reynek's visual art, which was put on in Prague in Spring 2014, and which was criticized by many friends of Reynek's family. But even this mass-oriented, commercialized, and at times kitsch phase of Reynek's mythicization did not decrease the force of his work.

Even when he is thus retrospectively placed in the mainstream, he still remains a poet who offers alternatives: for those who view the modern period as one of ever accelerating technological advancement, mounting chaos, and hectic civilization – a poet in his archaic, simple world, with his animals, and slow rhythms of the rural day and liturgical year; for those who view the modern period as one of almost mandatory politically engaged poetry, whether on this side or that – a poet utterly independent of politics; for those who view the modern period as one of effete and over-ripe avant-gardes and a literature too proud of its own obscurities – a poet of old-world rhymed simplicity, at times almost naïve, a poet writing easily memorized, lapidary rhymes, poem-prayers; for those who view the modern period as one of suppressed anxiety – a poet who confesses his anxiety; for those who view the modern period as one of a search for spirituality, but at the same time distrust ecclesiastic institutions – a poet deeply spiritual and anchored in tradition, but still experiencing it personally, for, as we have noted, Reynek's liturgy takes place, not in the church, but in the landscape.

Martin C. Putna

Toward the end of his life Bohuslav Reynek published a poem that was uncharacteristic in two respects. Its last couple of words are French and Greek. Some poets prosper at the edges of their language, and import foreign words, but Reynek was not one of them. Most of his poetry remains lexically within Czech, with the exception of Biblical vocabulary that had long been domesticated in many European languages over the past millennium (and this is also the case of the Greek word, Lethe, the last in the poem). There are many contrasts between, say, Edward Thomas and T. S. Eliot, and their respective approaches to lexicon are indicative of other differences. Whereas Eliot ranges almost promiscuously through foreign languages, Thomas goes deeper into English word hordes, intuiting their connection with the land he walks over and the air he breathes. The French word Reynek uses is *lait*.

This presents little difficulty even to a reader with no French, and the poem itself provides prompts. In deciding not to use the Czech word *mléko* (cognate with our English *milk*), he steps outside his language, into another. Translators sometimes remark that simple words can be the most difficult to translate. Walter Benjamin's example is how French *pain* denotes a very different set of experiences from the German *Brot*. They taste differently, they are obtained in different ways and in different settings; and so, as we break their different crusts, we feel and taste all the aspects that distinguish life in a Francophone community from a Germanophone one. Mutlu Konuk Blasing also emphasizes the way that the phonemes themselves feel differently as we pronounce them, which connects with our somatic history, as our mouths learned the word while eating the food, or in this case of "Rue L...," drinking the liquid.[1] Reynek obviously sensed that the Czech word for *milk* was insufficient at this last moment of the poem. As a translator, he had spent a lot of his working life demonstrating that his mother tongue could find terms for anything in French or German. But here that mastery is dropped or

---

[1] Mutlu Konuk Blasing, *Lyric Poetry: The Pain and The Pleasure of Words* (Princeton: Princeton University Press, 2007), 7–8.

found wanting: he does not translate the word, as something, or someone, stops him.

His connection with France was not only literary, and this brings us to the second uncharacteristic aspect of the poem. On March 13, 1926, he married the French poet Suzanne Renaud (1889–1964) in Grenoble. They would later have two sons, Jiří and Daniel, and from the outset of World War II, spent their lives in Czechoslovakia on a farmstead in the village of Petrkov, in the Czech-Moravian Highlands, about an hour-and-a-half's drive south-east of Prague. His wife pined for her homeland the more she aged. It is a thousand kilometers between their birthplaces, and from 1939 to 1945, and again, from 1948 to the ends of their lives, military and political conflicts made the journey impossible. Yet this journey – whether undertaken or prevented – was constitutive of their life together. Though cosmopolitan in his interests, engaging with French and German poetry in the original, he was always uneasy spending longer periods away from home, even when staying in Grenoble, which he frequently did before the war.

Their children grew up bilingually, and would continue their father's work of translation and publication of French literature. Reynek translated his wife's work into Czech and they met when he was translating her first book of poems, *Ta vie est là* (1922); in English, Your Life is Here. (The subsequent years would give an ironic shade to this title, as it turned out that her life was not, indeed, "here" in Grenoble, but "there," in Czechoslovakia.) The poem's title, "Rue L...," refers to rue Lesdiguières, where the Renaud family had an apartment. While Reynek is one of the most compelling poets of the spirit, exploring the ways in which humans are connected to both the things of this world and of another, it is rare for him to make a poem depend on biographical information like this.

"Rue L..." begins with children wandering through the street, as dawn approaches. They are going for milk and bring their coins with them. The liminal moment between night and day reminds the poet that they are also on another threshold, between life and what comes after. The coins they hold might, in the end, be handed over to Charon, and not the milk man. The shades of the underworld contrast with the whiteness of the life-giving liquid. Reynek concludes by turning away from the children to address his wife, Suzanne, as they pick up some coins also:

We'll take these on long roads,
entranced, across the lea,
round waters and through woods,
whispering: *lait*, Lethe...

As with the children, the couple may find both earthly and unearthly uses for the coins. Because they are agèd, they stand even closer to the threshold of life than the children. He also figures a more literal journey, through the lands that separate France and Czechoslovakia. Tolls are paid *in specie* for different types of journeys.

Reynek was also a Catholic. While much has been written on the cross fertilization of literature in the first decades of the twentieth century with religious beliefs from Judaism to Theosophy, we are less accustomed to Roman Catholicism. For this, we must look to French writers such as Paul Claudel, Charles Péguy, and Léon Bloy, among others. Reynek's engagement with this intellectual current was profound, and he often adopted its apocalyptic contours in his early career. His home in Petrkov, both biographically and poetically, was underwritten by far-flung places, long journeys, and foreign languages. His life, like that of his wife, although intimately connected with one place, was really everywhere.

His Catholic faith and his farm are the two important frames for both his life and his art. Some poets excel at showing us the complex extent of the world; others look no further than their gardens. Reynek belongs to the latter category: in his greatest poems he remains within the bounds of the farmstead in Petrkov, observing the livestock, the light, and the seasons. His Christian faith makes this space infinite. He finds no easy scriptural lessons in his experience, neither does he impose any. Indeed, on occasion his faith deepens his despair (and then vice versa). For Reynek there is no tension between the physical phenomena he records and the chasms and exaltations of the spiritual life. These are instinct with one another. No ideas but in things? Reynek might well respond: *only* ideas in things? What about – as another American poet put it – the heavens, the hells, the worlds, the longed-for lands? These too can be perceived in the things of this world, if only one attends carefully enough. His poems are true records of what he saw, and they do not exclude marvels.

For many people, vast gulfs separate the physical world they perceive and the realm of spirit. Organized religions insert ecclesiastic institutions, edifices, garments, and ceremonies between these zones, paradoxically in order to make them closer. Such mediation works for some people, and alienates others. Although Reynek belonged to the first group, the startling thing about so much of his poetry is that it demonstrates simply, briefly, and persuasively the proximity of the body, the ground, the trees, the bricks, the animals – all the physical stuff around us – to spirit. No mediation is required; the poet simply states what he touches and sees, and all is revealed, or at least as much as humankind is capable of absorbing.

The work of translating Bohuslav Reynek into English was undertaken as much out of love for his poems as it was fueled by the intuition that anglophone poetry at the moment may be curious about new ways to talk about the spirit. During a period when the Roman Catholic church is deservedly in the stocks, and will most likely remain there for the foreseeable future, Reynek is untimely. Yet he does not come as an advocate for that church, but as the poet of those moments, the angles, the shades when spirit is revealed in things. For him, this led along a path to the church portico, but many of his readers will probably prefer to linger longer with Reynek in the yard, observing the evening coming on, deleting the solid substances of things, and in the process revealing hairline cracks, strips of shade, fissures, and protuberances, where the physical world doesn't quite add up, vouchsafing us glimpses of things beyond.

Wordsworth would have called these "spots of time"; more generally, the Romantic tradition refers to them as the sublime, when we stand on the threshold of what we know and glimpse large forces beyond. Much of this was communicated in ecstatic apostrophes on mountain-tops, storm-beaten shores, and opium-tinted Asiatic vistas. It was also accompanied by a cult of the poet's personality, in which Romantic poets told stories about themselves, to set off the expanses beyond them. Although he works with the same disruptive material, Reynek is calmer, as he effortlessly commutes between this world and the next. His spiritual access, underwritten by Roman Catholicism, rather emerges out of centuries-long continuities of image, word, song, and ceremony.

A poet like Reynek appears in English, as though out of nowhere, and we scramble for some explanatory context. The first resort of many anglophone readers will probably be the Cold War, and they will be curious about how Reynek relates to, say, Miroslav Holub, and perhaps poets from neighboring countries such as Czesław Miłosz, Zbigniew Herbert, and Hans Magnus Enzenberger. Yet this is of scant use. Simply put, the Czechoslovak regime was not discernible from the window in Petrkov. Not that the authorities left Reynek alone; they nationalized the farmstead in 1949 (though they allowed him and his family to live and work on it). From 1948, Communist cultural commissars had instituted a critical practice of strategic amnesia, designating texts, music, paintings, and films that had no socialist ambitions as non-art. When the regime relaxed somewhat in the 1960s, during the Prague Spring, many poets and intellectuals visited Reynek in the Czech-Moravian Highlands to pay homage. Restitution and remembrance were integral to liberalization, and Reynek, as both artist and poet, was valued by the younger generation, in part because he unwittingly treated Communism in kind, designating it as a non-subject, not important enough to mention in his poems, or to depict in his paintings.

If not the Cold War, then what? "Rue L..." offers another context. Foreignness was integral to this most Czech of poets from the outset. Tradition had it that the family name came from France or Spain. Dagmar Halasová writes that they "based their claim on an entry in a register, where the oldest known Reynek of their family, Jakub, is given as 'Reňk,' the inverted circumflex above the letter *n* a residue of the Spanish *tilde*. The name itself, they said, then came from the adjective *renco*, or lame."[2] Halasová, like most other critics, demurs, but that the family wished to claim such an origin is interesting in itself.

Reynek went to high school in the nearby town of Jihlava, or in German, Iglau. Whereas the present day Czech Republic is monoglot, up to 1945 it was more cosmopolitan, and one contributing factor was that German was the first language of over three million people (almost 30% of the Czech and Moravian population), known as *Deutschböhmen*, or Sudeten Germans. Jihlava was a predominantly German-speaking town,

---

[2] Dagmar Halasová, *Bohuslav Reynek* (Brno: Petrov, 1992), 9.

with a large Jewish community. In 1914 Reynek began working with Josef Florian, a publisher with modest means and large ambitions. A Roman Catholic also, he was drawn to French contemporary writers (he was also the first to publish J. M. Synge and W. B. Yeats in Czech). From the small town of Stará Říše, he commissioned translations, often by Reynek, and published the works in fine editions that frequently amazed French authors when they received copies, with exotic frank marks, in the post.

He was not the only Czech publisher intensely interested in foreign writers, and many of these translations had a transformative effect on Czech literature in the period. Having long engaged with German-language writing, Czech authors were renewing their interest in France, from the Catholic conservatism that Reynek and Florian were involved with, to André Breton, whose Prague connections would later play an integral role in the history of surrealism. In the 1920 and 1930s, Reynek himself translated works by Paul Valéry, Francis Jammes, Georg Trakl, Jean Giono, Charles Baudelaire, Paul Claudel, Charles Péguy, Rainer Maria Rilke, Jules Amédée Barbey d'Aurevilly, Adalbert Stifter, Victor Hugo, Marcel Schwob, Charles d'Orléans, Georges Bernanos, Léon Bloy, Jean de la Fontaine, and Paul Verlaine, among many others. It was an extraordinary achievement. Naturally, his engagement with some writers was deeper than others, and, as critics agree, Reynek came into his own as a poet in this period, with the publication of *Lip by Tooth* in 1925.

Perhaps he found himself through others; perhaps he needed to hear strange sounds in German and in French in order to discover a way of writing in Czech. Radek Malý remarks that Reynek was not purely a servant of other authors in his translations, but left the unmistakable imprint of his own poetic personality on the work.[3] Translation theory has long argued about the ethics of such exchanges, and there is something suspicious about writers using foreign texts as occasions to flaunt their own particular styles, on occasion without knowledge of the source language. Here we have a different phenomenon, as the style and imagination of the poet-translator is expanded by the foreign materials, even as it pushes back against them.

---

[3] Radek Malý, *Příběhy básní a jejich překladů* [The Stories of Poems and Their Translations] (Olomouc: Vydavatelství Filozofické fakulty Univerzity Palackého, 2014), 61.

Malý follows the remarkable path of translations of Arthur Rimbaud into German, and their subsequent influence on both German and Czech poetry. These translations enjoyed huge success and Georg Trakl was their ardent admirer. Karl Klammer, the translator, took many freedoms in phrasing and image; the versions were often riffs on Rimbaud rather than literal renderings, and these affected Trakl's work directly. This was striking, as Trakl had good French and could have read the originals. Next, Trakl is translated into Czech by Reynek, often preserving Klammer's coinages. Through them Trakl became one of the most influential foreign poets on Czech poetry in the period between the wars. Malý remarks that "it is paradoxical that what readers today perceive as motifs and metaphors specific to Trakl in many cases come from Rimbaud, or rather from Karl Klammer and the way that he translated Rimbaud into German."[4] This leads him to the conclusion that translators of poetry are not always neutral mediums, but can initiate and inform new relations between and within traditions. In English, while we have some experience of foreign influence on the language's poetry (though not as extensive as most other European languages), we overlook the role of translators. In the case of most Eastern European poetry, this is justified, given their relatively small creative input (Holub is a good example of this). On closer inspection, we see that translators, often unacknowledged and uncredited, are important nodes in the translingual networks that make up the European poetic tradition, contributing to its themes and contours. At home in Petrkov, tending to his goats, observing the snow on the yard, the cattle in the byre, a long way from Prague's cafés and bars where writers worked out their differences, Reynek stood at the very centre of this continental system.

Klammer's involvement, the extent of its influence unacknowledged prior to Malý's study, is an index of the deeper and wider patterns of what is sometimes referred to as World Literature. This term is too large for our present purpose; the European zone is sufficiently capacious and labyrinthine. It is a centuries-long conversation across borders and languages, intense in some directions, slack in others, exchanging these valencies from decade to decade. Because English has been a lingua franca for almost seventy years now, and because it has a good chance of main-

---

[4] Malý, *Příběhy*, 55.

taining that status for a few more decades, we tend to miss these kinds of conversations, even though they were constitutive of our own poetic tradition, for instance in sixteenth-century sonneteering.

In his essay here, Martin C. Putna looks at some of the different forms and modes of Christian literature in Europe in the past centuries, in order to define the Czech approach in the early twentieth century. In the English tradition, two of the finest poets of religious poetry are Gerard Manley Hopkins and George Herbert. Both are at the heart of the English tradition of devotional poetry; both are intensely engaged with form. Hopkins on occasion pushes words to their limits. Donald Davie remarked that such contortions damaged the poems, but others have not agreed; for instance, Seamus Heaney found in Hopkins expressive possibilities that opened him, Heaney, as a poet. Similarly, the critic Miroslav Červenka has referred to the "cloddishness," or "ineptitude" of Reynek's language, not as negative criticism, but rather as a means of identifying Reynek's rejection of poetic speech that has been smoothed and sleekly shaped by the current in the centre of the stream.[5] Putna elsewhere identifies this as Reynek's deliberate turn from both "text-book prosody and the avant-garde" to embrace a linguistic knottiness and naivety.[6] Other poets who come to mind are Robert Frost and Edward Thomas, for their use of form and the rural setting of many of their poems.

But comparison only gets us so far, and the similarities observed can often be of an aleatory nature, too general to be illuminating, as though we claim a similarity between the practice of crystal gazing and the game of soccer because they both use a ball. Roman Catholicism, as a common factor between Hopkins and Reynek, is different from this, as it is a shared European heritage, both a framework of belief and a tradition of cultural artifacts. The same holds for the tradition of European lyric poetry, some of its skeins tweezed out by Malý above. By remembering how many foreign debts anglophone poetry has accrued over the centuries of

---

[5] In Czech, Červenka uses the word *neohrabanost*, "Bestiář Bohuslava Reynka" [Bohuslav Reynek's Bestiary], in *Styl a význam* [Style and Significance] (Prague: Československý spisovatel, 1991), 79.

[6] Martin C. Putna, "Proměny neměnného" [Metamorphoses of the Unchanging], in *Bohuslav Reynek: pieta v lodce / pietà dans la barque*, ed. Věra Jirousová (Prague: Památník národního písemnictví, 2002), 67.

its existence – from Greek, Latin, Italian, French poetry among others – we are reminded that a poet like Reynek, who seems to emerge from a faraway country of which we know little, is part of the same tradition, of which English poems are only one part. This is lyric poetry of a type in which the poet uses certain patterns of rhyme and pacing that many previous generations have. It is a way of finding likenesses in both words and the world, or sometimes impressing phonic likenesses on disparate experiences, and savoring the phases of that difference.

Successful poetry translation – and Reynek was very successful – reminds us of this common European tradition. Rimbaud arrives with éclat in German, transforming Trakl, who then is brought into Czech, helping Reynek at a key moment in his poetic development. Reynek now approaches English, trailing these particular clouds from French and German skies, as well as Latin, Italian, and of course Czech. Successful poetry translation often also hides the work of conveyance, the long hours spent learning another language, and then the months and years spent becoming familiar with alien airs and graces. We overlook translators in our enthusiastic discovery that we have much in common with a poet from another language. This is what Reynek did when rendering Jammes, Trakl, and many others into Czech, and it is also what he did in his original work, as he mostly excludes the traces of foreign, as I mentioned at the outset, rejecting a macaronic modernist technique in favor of the unadulterated mother tongue.

This is why "Rue L..." is such an intriguing poem, as it hints at the long journey that translation requires; it also indicates that translation not only entails the transfer of literal content and rhymes from one language to another – a kind of advanced crossword-puzzle work – but is connected with friendships, marriages, children, systems of belief, and personal fates. Milk is the first thing that most human beings taste; at the same time they also taste the flesh of another person. Soon after this, they learn their mother tongue, which is both a symbolic code and a matrix of physical sensations. We are physically situated in a language – the coding carved in our oldest bodily memories. No matter how fluent we become in other languages, we are anchored thus in our first words. The word *lait* remains recalcitrantly untranslated, in acknowledgement both of his wife, as well as the limits of his own mastery as translator.

In the translations of this book I have tried to naturalize Reynek as much as possible in English. On occasion, I have not resisted the temptation to make him echo Frost and Thomas, as I feel that they are germane to him, as indicated above. For the most part I have replicated his rhyme schemes, though I have not done the same for his meters. The most natural measures in Czech poetry are trochaic and dactylic, often in alexandrines. Dactyls are difficult to use in English outside light verse, and the extra foot of an alexandrine can make a line unwieldy. Rather I have sought equivalent devices – pentameter for alexandrine, iambic for trochaic. This approach can be executed with minimum sacrifice of paraphrasable content in poems with longer lines, but when the lines have a mere four to six syllables, the translator has less room for maneuver than the poet. Nevertheless, I persisted in the attempt to domesticate him in English, a language Reynek could not read.

I mentioned above the occasional, deliberate awkwardness of Reynek's language. Because Czech is an inflected language, a lot of the information that English puts in articles, prepositions, and pronouns, is encoded within verbs and nouns themselves. Thus, in fewer syllables, Czech, like most Slavic languages, can express more than English. Poets have seen the obvious advantages of this. But even for Czech poetry, Reynek forges his lines with extraordinary compression, on occasion making it difficult for native speakers to work out the syntactical relations. This allows Reynek to slow readers down in some places (and then in others, he lets them glide unhindered). Because this technique arises out of the grammatical nature of Czech, it is difficult to reproduce in English. What I have tried to do on occasion is to blur the syntactic relations of certain clauses to the rest of the sentence. There may be two possibilities, or even three. Such moments should serve as pauses, brief puzzlements that will ultimately dissolve in the discourse of the poem in its entirety.

Another device that creates equivalence is allusion. As remarked above, here and there Reynek in English may seem to echo anglophone poets whose work he didn't know. What justifies such an approach? We read foreign writers for a variety of reasons: sometimes we want to be assured that far-flung cultures and people are, fundamentally, the same as us; sometimes we want to hear something that is irrefutably alien; and sometimes, most bizarrely and most usually, we read them for both of these reasons at once. It may irritate some readers to encounter such familiarizing devices, like finding ketchup in our satay. However, we often associate food with particular cultures and not others, occluding the promiscuous journeys that dishes have always travelled. (Ketchup, like satay, comes from Malaysia.) It is my hope that such allusions and overtones in the translations gesture toward deeper commonalities, indicating how Reynek belongs to the European lyric tradition. Mere wishful thinking it may be, but wishes work best when they cleave to reality: I would like to think that, through Francis Jammes and others, he could see Frost and Thomas as kindred spirits.

And, of course, maybe not. Translators always come to their material with a set of tastes and inclinations – some might say with an agenda – and this governs both the choice of work to be translated and the way it is done. The translators I most admire leave shades of their own in the work. Sometimes these are minimal; sometimes substantial. To adapt Wordsworth, the good translator half creates and half perceives. The bad translator also half creates and half perceives, but the timing is always wrong.

It is only fair, then, to give the anglophone reader an idea of the way in which these translations have altered the Czech primary material. The kind of freedom I mean can be demonstrated by the poem, "Sticks in a Fence." The last four lines in my translation go as follows:

> These lean, long years your bony shanks,
> waiting, locked in leas.
> Burls in palms, heels in mud-banks.
> You don't have any knees.

Here is the original:

> Hubených let holé hnáty
> do čekaní zajaté.
> Suky v dlaních. V hlíně paty.
> Kolena nemáte.

This could be literally translated as follows:

Bare limbs of lean years
imprisoned in waiting.
Burls in palms. Heels in mud.
You have no knees.

I translated backwards from the final lines, since in my view the clear declarative force of lines 3 and 4 had to be preserved above all. These do not only end a stanza, but the entire poem. Thus, I granted myself leeway translating the literal meaning of lines 1 and 2. But the important question is how much and in what way. In the first line of the original, the alliterative aspirate was important and is replicated in the four liquids of lines 1 and 2. The idea of imprisonment is replicated in "locked," but that means introducing the word "leas," which is absent from the original stanza. Yet it is implicit in the scene of the poem. Moreover, the slight archaism of the English word compensates for other places in the translations where I was unable to replicate Reynek's older usages. I have also created a kind of syntactic dissonance to match that of the Czech. "Bony shanks" does service for limbs, and may seem too ornate for the original, but here I was trying to catch a particular ironic usage of *hnáty* in Czech, and this precipitated a slight change at the end of line 3, in order to accommodate the rhyme.

Indubitably, some readers will feel that, here or elsewhere, I have taken too many liberties with literal meaning. I offer the above example not in the hope of mitigating such judgements; rather I wish to emphasize that translation is firstly interpretation. The decision to convey intact the literal meaning of some lines rather than others is made on the basis of an understanding of the poem, an interpretation, that might not be shared by others. There is never an objective crib that everyone can agree on, to which translators then apply their different stylings.

In any case, the above gives an idea of some of the tolls incurred by Reynek as he fares from Czech to English. It is a long way to travel between the two languages, and there are many dark passages on the road. He is an unlikely and untimely guest to find at the door. May his welcome be no less warm for that.

Justin Quinn

Some artists excel both in the visual arts and in literature. Usually those gifts are unequal, but in rare cases we find it difficult to say which muse has the upper hand. In the Czech Republic, Bohuslav Reynek belongs to this smaller group. While his poetic oeuvre stretches roughly over his entire life – most intensely in his young years, and later more measured – his art displays striking swings and developments, metamorphosing over time in relation to the poems. There is little evidence of Reynek's artistic talent in his early youth – only about thirty drawings of his home, at the farmstead in Petrkov village and its surroundings, and the oldest group from his time at high school in the nearby town of Jihlava.

His development as an artist was markedly slower than as a poet. He studied at the Jihlava school under Max Eisler, an erudite young professor who gathered around him a circle of students, teaching them about art in more theoretical than practical terms, commenting in passing on their extracurricular artistic activities. Thus, Reynek was mostly self-taught. Still, Reynek was interested at an early stage about developments in contemporary art: for instance, he had a subscription in the bookshop at Jihlava to the progressive art magazine *Open Paths*, which he read carefully. At that time, the magazine was attentive to the new movement of Expressionism, which had originated in Germany and later spread northward; contrasting with Impressionism, Naturalism, and Academicism, it emphasized personal feeling and experience, resisting the conventions of their representation. The earliest preserved examples of Reynek's pictures, mainly from around 1910, breathe with this spirit of Expressionism. While many of the accompanying drawings mentioned above from this period are diligent and determined studies of nature, as yet they tell us nothing about Reynek's artistic potential. After 1914, his hectic literary activity pushed the artist in him far into the background. For this is when Reynek encountered Stará Říše.

This village was about 100 kilometers south of Reynek's Petrkov, and near Jihlava, where he spent his student years. Influenced by the ideas of the French philosopher, Léon Bloy, a local high-school teacher, Josef Florian, founded a Catholic-oriented publishing house, Dobré dílo (Good

Work), which released over 400 books and journals under his direction. Here after 1914 Reynek found a publisher for his early poems as well as his translations from French and German; he also became a frequent contributor to Florian's journal, *Nova et vetera*. Along with excerpts of work by French and German poets, Reynek was also able to explore his ideas about art, if only on a theoretical level, in a series of translated studies of various European artists (among others, Paul Gauguin, Vincent van Gogh, Edvard Munch, Marc Chagall, and Emil Nolde). Stará Říše's activities were firmly grounded in the visual arts: the books published by Dobré dílo were exquisitely designed. Also, *Nova et vetera* regularly devoted several pages to the visual arts. Along with various Medieval woodcuts and reproductions of old passion scenes and stained glass tableaux, we also find reproductions of eminent European artists. Several lesser known Czech artists are to be found there. Although in his first letters to Stará Říše he characterized himself primarily as a visual artist, he was patently caught up in literary work and various editorial activities, and had only a single illustration in Dobré dílo's publications in 1914 – a pen drawing of the Archangel Michael in a book by Paul Féval, *La Fée des Grèves*.

In 1918, however, Reynek's work with Stará Říše brought him into contact with two seasoned artists, whom he had already encountered in the journals *Open Paths* and *Artists' Monthly* during his years in Jihlava. They were Vlastislav Hofman and Josef Čapek (brother of the writer, Karel Čapek), exponents of Modernism in contemporaneous Czech art; Čapek moreover was a member of the already well-known group Tvrdošíjní (The Obstinates). He provided about forty illustrations for Reynek's translation of Francis Jammes's novel *Le Roman du lièvre* (French publication 1903), which appeared with Dobré dílo in 1920. Čapek's collection, *Eight Linocuts*, had already been published there the previous year. Hofman also published the linocut cycle, *Heads* (1920), and in the same year his *Christu, Madonna, and the Saints*, inspired by Ethiopian motifs. All this must have contributed to Reynek's decision. The wider audience that Florian had already provided him with as a poet, translator, and literary critic, might be within reach for him as an artist also; thus on his first meeting with Hofman, he inquired about linocut chisels. Hofman sent some straightaway.

Reynek had now, at last, moved beyond his apprenticeship as an artist, which is clear from thirty-five linocuts of fairly high quality. He produced these in one burst, which we can follow in detail through his correspondence with Josef Florian during 1920. When this phase ended, he decided to send the best rural scenes to Josef Čapek; perhaps at the back of his mind he was thinking of that artist's urban scenes, albeit his own were in a smaller format. His linocuts were, as was often the custom in Stará Říše's productions, also hand-colored. They included biblical scenes, and Reynek's remarkable Isaiah figure displays not only loose echoes of Čapek, but also the more intimate inspiration of Georges Rouault, whom Florian had published some years before in a representative selection of color collotypes (several originals by the French artist also hung on the walls of his home).

Čapek was famed for his elegant treatment of the graphic sign, but at the end of this linocut phase, Reynek's work manifests no such element. Perhaps he could not discipline his hands to the straight, bold lines. In his later work, Reynek sought a means of expression (like his work years later in drypoint and etching) that was more sensual and primitively robust, the forms almost trembling and blurred. Unlike the rational Cubist Čapek, Reynek, just turned thirty, was an Expressionist, which he would remain for the rest of his life. What perhaps began as a shortcoming, ended up being one of Reynek's great strengths.

In 1923 Reynek saw a collection of poems, *Ta vie est là*, by an unknown French poet, Suzanne Renaud, in the window of a Prague bookshop. This would change his life. He immediately translated it, and contacted the Grenoble author. He would marry her three years later. After that they began commuting annually between Grenoble for the winter and Petrkov for the summer. At this time Reynek decided definitively on the vocation of artist. Even at the outset, when he began working with Stará Říše on a freelance basis as a writer and artist, he knew that he would have to earn money from these pursuits. He was too proud to ask his parents, the owners of the Petrkov farmstead, to support his artistic interests. But despite his intense work rate, which was for him unprecedented, the honorariums for his poetry and translations were insufficient for even the bare necessities of married life, especially since the couple soon had children to think of. On their wedding announcement, we read that the groom's profession is the grand-sounding *homme de lettres*; the designation *peintre* did not figure there at all. Marriage to Renaud changed this: it was the other side of Reynek's talent that could provide best for the family. But his feverish total engagement in literary activities for Stará Říše put his work as an artist on the backburner, with the exception of a year when he produced over thirty small linocuts. Apart from these, in the *catalogue raisonné* of the artist's early work we find little or nothing.

Soon, during the summer after his wedding, he produced a large number of pastels of French and Czech landscapes; reports of his extraordinarily intense artistic work, which Reynek was sending to his friend and publisher Vlastimil Vokolek, every few months. In Fall 1927, the Grenoble journal *La vie Alpine* printed a review of Reynek's exhibition of the time. And early the next year, Reynek took part in a large Grenoble show which "included all the well-known Parisians."[1] His works hung there next to two other Czechs – Otakar Kubín and Jiří (Georges) Kars; the French or France-based artists he was confronted with included Albert Marquet, Kees van Dongen, Maurice Utrillo, Maurice de Vlaminck, Marcel Gromaire, André Lhote, André Derain, and others. It was not a bad start. He now came into contact not only with French literati such as Beranos, but also visual artists whose work he sent back to Czechoslovakia to supplement his literary activities (woodcuts by R. S. Bechetoille to accompany his translation of Paul Valéry's "Le cimetière marin"). In Grenoble Reynek also became close friends with Gabriel Ducultit, the artist, and he struck up an acquaintance with the art expert André Farcy, director of the graphic-art department in the museum there, which was the first to purchase Reynek's French works, and offered informed commentaries on his exhibitions. In the mild Grenoble winters, the artist would set out from the busy city (which he disliked) with his charcoals and pastel chalks for the Poisat area, which suited him much better. He enjoyed scaling the Alpine slopes and going through its vineyards near Grenoble, to paint the autumnal atmospheres of Dauphiné and other small churches. At this time he also developed a special love for the gently rugate Provence, similar to his home in the Czech-Moravia Highlands. In Manosque he befriended the writer Jean Giono, and would be the first to present the Frenchman to Czechs in translation.

---

[1] Letter to Vlastimil Vokolek, January 3, 1928. In Bohuslav Reynek, *Korespondence* [Correspondence], ed. Jiří Šerých and Jaroslav Med (Prague: Karolinum Press, 2012), 467.

In 1929, he exhibited the fresh harvest of his pastels and drawings in a show that Vlastimil Vokolek organized in the Municipal Museum of Pardubice. His first exhibition in Czechoslovakia, it revealed France, more than his homeland, as the fundamental catalyst for his artistic activity. At that time, perhaps to his own pleased amazement, he became aware of a shift in his status: "I'm translating very little at the moment (even when the opportunity arises) – art has taken all my love over literary pursuits – they seem to alternate..."[2]

Reynek's artistic work from the mid-1920s to the mid-1930s did not reflect his deep bond with Christianity. From the viewpoint of his later copper-plate prints, which dealt with spiritual subjects, several art critics view the drawings and paintings of Reynek's interwar period as undistinguished, even going as far as to identify it as conservative. Granted, it was overly thematic and formally unadventurous (especially, in the Czech context, where Cubism had long been established and Surrealism was taking hold). Now, however, Reynek was surprisingly apathetic toward these isms, especially given his sympathies with those representatives of Czech Modernism, who had earlier so impressed him, among these Čapek and Hofman.

Although there is not enough space here for a wider evaluation of this period, it is clear that the pastels executed in Dauphiné and Provence, as well as in his native Petrkov, possess the kind of "simplification that leads to synthesis,"[3] whether they display a loose, magisterially colored, prodigious execution, bordering on Fauvism, or whether they employ a delicate, characteristically sensitive observation of details that never devolves into mere description. Also in his charcoal drawings we find the same synthesis through the whole spectrum of his work of the time, from the frailest lines to the darkest material emphases in the service of remarkably poetic landscapes, unlike those of any other Czech artist.

Reynek had plans for a portfolio of drawings of French and Czech chapels, as well as of pastures and field work, using halftone printing. At that time, the technique was still not fully developed, and the plans were doomed to fail. Nevertheless, this attempt only further strengthened

---

[2] Unpublished letter to Vlastimil Vokolek, July 15, 1929. Museum of Czech Literature.
[3] Letter to Josef Florian, December 28, 1927. In Reynek, *Korespondence*, 216.

his resolve to master the printing processes on his own. What he need-ed above all was a step-by-step description of the process by which he could learn drypoint technique. In the winter of 1932, his printer friend, Vlastimil Vokolek sent at his request an illustrated manual to Grenoble. Because Reynek didn't want to wait for the following summer in Petrkov to make a start, he ordered a small, unfussy machine press from Prague. So, as with his earliest drawings when he was attending high school in Jihlava, now years later he taught himself by depicting those domes-tic objects nearest him, the interiors of forests and lone pine-trees, the fields with corn and barley mows after the harvest, as well as the bend of paths through fields and along the shores of ponds. These works also try to capture as accurately as possible the atmospheres and moods of summer, and later – when his trips to France came to an end – of winter also. Even at this stage, the artist turned his gaze downward to the tiny details of nature, just as he had earlier programmatically taught himself to do in his drawings (thus we see in his work clusters of grain as well as foxglove flowers and studies of spiders and moths on birch leaves). With ever greater success and care he came nearer to the intimate corners of his own house and his native village. But something fundamental was still to occur.

Only with the onset of war, after a long phase of painting (that re-flected global events) did Reynek once more muster his courage to return to Florian's ideas, that is, to embrace a spiritual dimension in his art, an aspect that was already so manifest in hundreds of lines of his own poet-ry, for instance in the collections, *Fish Scales* (1922), *Lip by Tooth* (1925), and *The Sowing of Solitude* (1936). The first works – a series of "Escape to Egypt," "Birth of the Lord," "Mount of Olives," and the early series of "Calvary," etched from 1937 – were articulated into a number of smaller panels, somewhat like the stanzas of a poem (we can see this in "Eas-ter," 1938); others were of a somewhat artificially figural narrative nature, which broke up the overall compositional integrity, and as yet lacked the concentrated, synthesized later mode of expression. He began to master this – as well as achieve subtler gradations of technique – for the greater part in the ambitious monochrome cycle, "The Passion" (1941–49).

And so we come to the 1950s, a period that was as imaginatively re-warding for Reynek the artist, as it was anguished for Reynek the man.

One thing was clear to him from the outset: there was no way to continue the mystical realism and academic art of the preceding century, with its exhausted and hackneyed iconographic patterns, now fading throughout Europe. We may conjecture that one of the formal indicators of Reynek's new direction – even before he could himself carry out his graphic program – were the Chagall etchings for Gogol's *Dead Souls* (1923–27), which, in the mid-1930s, he could consider carefully at his leisure in the graphic collection of Grenoble Museum, where his friend Farcy worked. Chagall, even before he had begun his own work on the Bible, had much to teach Reynek in the use of the naive manner. Further inspiration – also welcome for its clean, naive style – could also have been the Romanesque murals and the stained glass in folk style, untethered from reality, which he saw in churches around Grenoble. A significant feature of the increasing sheets of work from the 1950s was that Reynek applied ever more colors over a monotype impression, applying finishing touches with a brush, thus making each print an original.

In his work of the 1950s Old Testament prophets and saints of the New Testament and later legend gaze out at us, some of them meditating, some in great pain. Then with the approach of the 1960s, his technique, while remaining brilliant, increasingly loses the earlier formal smoothness and orderliness. We see that the transparent and naïve faces are gradually etched with rougher contours, the material surface of the works themselves taking on aspects of the cruel and desperate situations these figures found themselves in. Finally it is as though the strong strokes of these tableaux, with their uncompromisingly expressive veins and capillaries, flowed directly from the hands of the artist.

However, the sacral remained only one part of the Reynek's work; in the other, he turned to more down-to-earth subjects of his home, its dark corners and hiding places, in still lifes depicting a wide range of unspeaking faces – among these the cats, sheep, turkeys, cocks, butterflies and moths that inhabited the yard and garden in Petrkov, as well as blue tits and other birds that suffered the frost beyond his window. He presents these as his fellow animals, God's creations like himself. Surprisingly, Reynek was slower to push these animals into abstraction; as he learned how to depict them with greater intimacy, he found the means to lift their tiny existences to higher levels of significance.

Does the category of Christian art restrict our idea of an artist and his achievement? From the long tradition of European art, we know that this is not the case. In his work, as in his life, Reynek was indubitably of that faith, aware instinctively of both how to lift all those living beings, powerless and without speech, from the earth heavenward and equally to bring the heavens as far as possible toward himself on the earth.

Jiří Šerých

CZECH TITLES OF ENGLISH POEMS

These translations are based on Milada Chlíbcová's edition of Reynek's poems, *Básnické spisy* (Zlín: Archa/Petrkov, 2009), and the Czech titles for the English translations are given below, with page numbers in this edition.

UNCOLLECTED POEM / 1925
A Fool / Blázen (623)

EARTH'S GRIEF / 1922 / SMUTEK ZEMĚ
Signs of Autumn / Tušení jeseně (103)

LIP BY TOOTH / 1925 / RTY A ZUBY
Hoar-Frost / Jíní (253)
Springtide / Vesna (255)
Ballad / Balada (263)
The Morning... / Ráno (265)
Pilgrimage to La Salette / Pouť na La Salettu (267)
Dawn in Winter / Svítání v zimě (269)
Idyll, Morning / Idyla jitřní (270)
Mid-Winter Longing / Stesk (273)
Three Goats / Kozlata (281)
Cockerels / Kohouti (283)
Carpenters in the Wind / Tesaři ve větru (287)
Hair / Vlasy (290)
Spider / Pavouk (291)
Fly / Moucha (292)

THE SOWING OF SOLITUDE / 1936 / SETBA SAMOT
Gathering Potatoes / Vybírání bramborů (311)
Yellow Bedstraw, a Blessing / Svízel (342)

LIST OF ILLUSTRATIONS

Illustrations from a private collection. Numbers in brackets correspond to the order in "Katalog výtvarného díla Bohuslava Reynka", in: *Bohuslav Reynek Katalog výstavy ke 100. výročí narození*, Vol. 2, ed. R. Bernardi, 1992-93.
Photographs on the cover and inside the book appear courtesy of the photographer, Dagmar Hochová.

TRANSLATOR'S ACKNOWLEDGEMENTS

Some of these translations first appeared in magazines and journals: *Blackbox Manifold, Causeway Magazine, Manchester Review, New Yorker,* and *Tower Poetry.* Many people gave help and advice along the way. At the outset, the poet's sons, Jiří and Daniel Reynek, offered encouragement. I would not have got very far without the help of my wife, Tereza Límanová, who advised on a wide range of matters, from grammar to greater issues of conveying Czech culture into English. Also, a number of people kindly read large sections of the book, saving me from myself on countless occasions; they are: Mike Baugh, Jakub Boguszak, David Grosser, Paul Ings, Peter McDonald, Daniel Soukup, Daniela Theinová, and Matouš Turek. I would also like to thank the following people: Petr Borkovec, Veronika Francová, Tomáš Fürstenzeller, Ernest Hilbert, Juraj Horváth, Josef Hrdlička, Kristina and Jiří Mědílek, Iva Mladičová, Štěpán Nosek, Petr Onufer, Ondřej Pilný, Kristina and Jan Roubal, Zuzana Říhová, Petr Šrámek, and Marek Toman.

NOTE ON THE TEXT
For these translations the following edition of Reynek's poems was used: *Básnické spisy,* ed. Milada Chlíbcová (Zlín: Archa/Petrkov, 2009).

PRAISE FOR BOHUSLAV REYNEK

Dear Mr. Reynek, You cannot know how much joy your poems brought to me – how their clarity and purity helped me... I must mention the unease, the admiration, that your verses evoked in my friends. When I told them your name, and the dates when some of the poems were written, they felt shame – the guilt one feels when he has no excuse for overlooking something, for sleeping through it.

Jiří Kolář, letter 29 June 1954, in BR: *Correspondence*

One of the giants of 20th century Czech poetry.

Michael Stein, *literalab: Central European Literary Life*

A goat by the road, a cat, and the winter landscape become everyday epiphanies in Bohuslav Reynek's gentle and profound poetry, rendered impressively here in Justin Quinn's translation.

Veronika Tuckerová, Harvard University, Department of Slavic Languages & Literatures

Goats, spiders, infernal roosters; a reddening sun, emerging florets; hayricks, byres, windows, rakes; Advent, Christmas; Job and Esau; the drama of sacrifice – these are poems attentive to, sprung from, a creaturely world subtended by a metaphysical presence. In Bohuslav Reynek the reader of English encounters a twentieth century Czech poet both profoundly Catholic and utterly, subtly modern.

Translator Justin Quinn has brought Reynek – himself an estimable translator of Rimbaud, Francis Jammes, Valéry – into an English aligned with the caretaking apparent directness of Frost, of Edward Thomas; other readers may hear here something of an Englished Georg Trakl. Earlier work channeling an often anguished energy gives way to something calmer, simultaneously sparer and more expansive.

There is a simplicity here as if of old ballads, folk songs – *as if*: this is the simplicity of the profoundly pondered, distilled, parsed and pared. Reynek's fly is, for example, an affine of Blake's. From his farmstead Reynek beheld the world. There seems here to be no need for a theory of objective correlatives: everything ingathered in the poet's work is always already allegorical, suffused, charged. Common rhythms and patterns – of season, of liturgical calendar, of sunrise and moonrise – inform the shapely forms of Reynek's poetry, a shapeliness Quinn has brought over into English.

Reynek might be seen as a *sentimentalische* in Schiller's sense, as opposed to naïve: "sentimental" in that his work has borne and transformed the burden of reflective consciousness, its working with deep and (formerly) common tropes a poetic ploughing of a simultaneously elemental and spiritual ground. In these selected poems we encounter an informed attentiveness, a sensibility alert to the signs and parables which the ordinary endlessly affords: baby goats who "usher in/the mundane in a vision," the "varicolored golds" of ploughed fields; sudden appearance of "Star prints of Paradise." One finds here not the effortfulness of epiphanies but the ongoing registration of a complex revelation: "So many stars in snow/and just one human track." It is timely for Reynek to have made his track into English. His work asks for, and rewards, a deep listening.

Maureen N. McLane, author of *This Blue* and *My Poets*, Professor of English at New York University

179

Bohuslav Reynek

THE WELL AT MORNING

KAROLINUM PRESS, Ovocný trh 560/5, 116 36 Praha 1,
Czech Republic
Karolinum Press is a publishing department of Charles University
www.karolinum.cz

Cover and graphic design by Jiří Voves
Photos and illustrations prepress František Nárovec
Typeset by DTP Karolinum
Printed in the Czech Republic by Těšínské papírny, s. r. o., Český Těšín
First English edition

ISBN 978-80-246-3452-8 (pb)
ISBN 978-80-246-3426-5 (ebk)

Colmar 1: octobre 1926

Mon cher grand — Quoique bien
attristée de notre séparation, j'
ait jusqu'à présent un bon v
sans aucun incident ; je ne
sens pas fatiguée ce matin
i par grand hasard je manqu
mon train de 7h. je pourrai
voir un à 13h½ qui m'amèn
rs 28h à Lyon. De toutes faço
is tranquille. Il y a beaucou
de jolies choses à Colmar, un
charme ancien et provincial
e plairait. A bientôt, mon
rand ; je pense à toi tout le
de cette visite aux églises et v
usées. Mon affectueux sou
ux tiens. Ne sois pas triste
trois baisers. Zozotte.